Master of Disaster

"This very talented maritime illustrator with his fine skillful insight and experience has produced works which have helped in the presentation and interpretation of maritime history."

-Shipwreck Journal

"Ed Pusick, Captain Ed, as we always called him, created masterpieces of shipwreck drawings."

–Dr. Charles E. Feltner and Jeri Baron Feltner –
Divers, Authors, and Shipwreck Historians

MASTER of DISASTER

The Life and Works of Shipwreck Artist Ed Pusick

Lois T. Hauck & Gary L. Hauck

iUniverse, Inc.
Bloomington

Master of Disaster
The Life and Works of Shipwreck Artist Ed Pusick

iUniverse books may be ordered through booksellers or by contacting:

iUniverse
1663 Liberty Drive
Bloomington, IN 47403
www.iuniverse.com
1-800-Authors (1-800-288-4677)

ISBN: 978-1-4759-8506-1 (sc)
ISBN: 978-1-4759-8507-8 (e)

Printed in the United States of America

iUniverse rev. date: 04/11/2013

To Ed

Table of Contents

Acknowledgements

We owe a debt of gratitude to those individuals and organizations who helped make this effort possible. First, we would like to thank the Great Lakes Shipwreck Historical Society for granting us permission to quote from articles, incorporate sketches, and include a full cover of the *Shipwreck Journal*. Individually, our thanks go to Sean Ley, Tom Farnquist, and Frederick Stonehouse, for their helpfulness, encouragements and support, as well as Fred's permission to use his term for Mr. Pusick – Master of Disaster (Stonehouse, 27 Jan. 2013). Special appreciation is offered to Mike McPharlin, Ed's mentor and friend, who willingly and enthusiastically granted us an interview, and loaned us Ed's personal portfolio that had been given him. We also wish to thank Dr. Charles E. Feltner and Jeri Baron Feltner for permission to include a photo of the front cover of their book titled *Shipwrecks of the Straights of Mackinac*.

On a more personal note, we are thankful for the time and technical assistance of our son, Jared, for electronically preparing the photos for the final manuscript.

To Dr. Maria Suchowski, our colleague and friend, we offer thanks for her willingness to proof read the manuscript and offer her valued feedback.

Carolyn Johnson, Visual Arts Coordinator of Montcalm Community College (MCC), and Debbie Bell, Adjunct Instructor of Visual Arts, are both given our thanks for their helpful commentary on Ed's works, and wonderful support of the Ed Pusick Gallery in their art building on MCC's Sidney campus.

Finally, we wish to thank each participating MCC art student for the permission granted to include his or her reflections on specific pieces within the Gallery.

Introduction

The Master of Disaster was Ed Pusick (1927 – 2006), a masterful illustrator whose works on Great Lakes Shipwrecks have been featured on the History Channel, displayed in museums, and gracing the covers of textbooks and journals on maritime tragedies.

A Navy veteran and disciple of draftsman Mike McPharlin, Ed has prolifically produced illustrations born of an architect's mindset and a Veteran's toughness, yet in touch with the naturalist's experiences of crashing waves and deep waters. In addition to formal graphics training and rich personal experience, he drew on many field consultations with ships' captains and divers, architects and historians in the production of works that faithfully capture crucial moments in the maritime record. His illustrations reflect the wealth of this diverse background.

Ed's works were also influenced by the writings and encouragements of Great Lakes shipwreck historian, Fred Stonehouse. Inside the front cover of Fred's own 1980 book on *Munising Shipwrecks* is his handwritten note, "Dear Ed, I hope you enjoy reading this. I know someday we will succeed in getting yours out."

But the story of the man behind the illustrations is equally intriguing. Between the years 1998 and 2006, Lois Hauck had the rare privilege of serving as his caregiver. During those years before his death, Ed shared with her much of his personal history, good humor, and stories behind his works. She had the privilege of traveling with him to maritime museums for the donation of limited edition prints, and witnessing many of these crucial conversations first-hand. Upon his death, she became the recipient of his correspondence and remaining works, now displayed in the Ed Pusick Gallery on the campus of Montcalm Community College in Sidney, Michigan. She is joined by her husband, Gary, a professor of humanities, in the compilation and writing of this account.

Ed Pusick
1927 - 2006

Chapter 1

Tender Heart, Skilled Hands

Ed Pusick (1927-2006) was born in Battle Creek, Michigan, and spent most of his career in West Michigan. His first tour of duty with the U.S. Navy provided a lesson in reality; but his love for the sea and ships brought him a second tour of duty in which he would suffer a permanent disability.

Ed felt that his calling to be an illustrator was due to an inborn trait. Ed's mother was a very talented watercolorist and portrait painter. Her lineage traced to seafarers and New England ship captains, including a U.S. Navy admiral. Ed's paternal uncle served as a commander in the U.S. Navy and later was a skipper of a large ocean freighter.

Pusick first worked as a nameplate decal artist and designer before his recall into active Navy duty in 1950 and it would be more than a quarter century before he was to render any kind of artwork again.

Mike McPharlin, a successful architect, became Ed's mentor and friend. Mike was a Great Lakes maritime history buff who believed Ed's creative skills should be applied to the many interesting historical vessels as subjects.

Ed's first series was 14 pastel renderings of sizable vessels lost in the Lakes. These pastels were mostly given away as gifts, and gave Ed the courage to test the waters of the donation exhibit area. His pictorial delineation technique led to a successful donation of his largest shipwreck illustration to the Michigan DNR in the fall of 1978.

Following this first series, Ed cranked out 14 more pastel renderings of shipwrecks. Two were donated to the Marquette Maritime Museum and about a dozen are in the Frederick Stonehouse Collection. (Fred Stonehouse, author of numerous books on Great Lakes shipwrecks, served on the Board of Directors for the museum and was the first to call Ed, "The Master of Disaster.") The pastel renderings proved to be an impractical method for promoting the mystery of Great Lakes shipwrecks. None tended to reflect the essence of *pure* shipwreck drama Ed witnessed as a young sailor boy.

It was then that Ed began experimenting or "doodling" with the pencil medium of expression. When Fred Stonehouse saw one of the small shipwreck doodles, he suggested that they (Ed and Fred) implement large pencil drawings in a series of limited edition print reproductions for Shipwrecks Unlimited Publishing. These drawings have now found their way into maritime museums across the country, and have been featured on The History Channel, in books, and in journals. The success of this method subsequently led to Ed's introduction to Tom Farnquist and the Great Lakes Shipwreck Historical Society (*Shipwreck Journal,* 1992: 4-7).

A limited number of prints of the Edmund Fitzgerald and a very limited number of larger prints are still available from the Grand Rapids Public Museum or the present writers.

The authors learned much about Ed Pusick, both the artist and the person, during the several years Lois worked as his caregiver. Shortly after Pusick's death, Tom Rademacker wrote the following article for *The Grand Rapids Press* titled, "Great ones not always appreciated until they're gone" (Sunday, 30 Apr. 2006: B1, B2):

> Ed Pusick's shipwreck art graced covers of books, brochures, more, but he was buried with little fanfare. Some of us chase fame and fortune as if they were our next breath of air. Then, there are artists such as Ed Pusick, of Wyoming [Michigan]. Over the last half of his 79-year life, Pusick drew and painted

scores of scenes depicting Great Lakes shipwrecks. His work graced the covers of books, brochures and newsletters. At least one of his renderings was cast in bronze, and his meticulous artwork was twice used to dramatize shipwreck documentaries on The History Channel.

But for all his work, Pusick – who earned the title "Master of Disaster" for his chilling illustrations of sinking vessels – never gained much status, nor sought it. His only sibling, a brother, died of polio at age 8. Pusick, a lifelong bachelor, spent the earlier parts of his life with his mother, then graduated to an apartment on 36th Street SW, where he lived alone.

The veteran of the U.S. Navy died April 7 [2006] and was buried four days later with military honors at Fort Custer in Battle Creek. An obituary in the Battle Creek Enquirer recalled nothing of how he dramatized the lore and legacy of shipwrecks littering the bottom of a nation's freshwater seas. 'He was a man who could capture every exciting detail before a ship went down,' said Tom Farnquist, executive director of the Great Lakes Shipwreck Historical Society. Farnquist had a long-running association with Pusick and solicited work from the artist for countless editions of the society's quarterly publication, 'Shipwreck Journal.'

'Early on, he was really the one we turned to if we wanted something special,' Farnquist said, noting Pusick was incredibly attentive to historical accuracy. 'There were other artists, but we had to coach them.'

Mike McPharlin befriended Pusick during the 1970's, when they worked for a local architectural firm. 'It's kind of sad,' McPharlin said of Pusick's unheralded death. 'I used to bird-dog for him a little, going up to the U.P. for research and clippings on shipwrecks. We'd try to pull everything together to make it as real as possible. Six months later, he'd have a picture.' And virtually every one of them made you glad to be out of a storm. With few exceptions, Pusick's works depict men on the brink of death.

- His rendition of 'The Edmund Fitzgerald in Storm' shows the 729-foot freighter being battered by 30-foot seas, just before its plunge to the bottom of Lake Superior on the night of Nov. 10, 1975.
- 'When Things Get Out of Hand' shows a schooner being ripped to shreds on an offshore reef.
- 'They Lost the Struggle' commemorates the unsolved double loss of the steamers Regina and Charles S. Price on Nov. 9, 1913.

Lois Hauck, of Plainfield Township, who provided home care for Pusick in part because he suffered from leg injuries sustained in the Navy, said her friend of eight years lived not only in anonymity, but modestly. He allowed himself one delicacy – imported cheese. Shortly before his death, Hauck said she caught Pusick throwing out a large collection of original artwork and prints. She fished them out of his trash, prompting him to ask her, 'What do you want with that crap?'

Hauck said Pusick once charged $1,300 for an original work of the Edmund Fitzgerald, but afterward developed ulcers [in his legs]. He chalked it up to 'The Curse of the Fitz' and never again took more than a few bucks for his work. His limited-edition prints rarely fetched more than $10 to $25 apiece. Most of his work, Hauck said, was donated to museums and given to individuals.

It was Lois Hauck who found the tall and lanky Pusick collapsed in his little apartment. She said he still felt warm, and she tried unsuccessfully to resuscitate him with CPR. It seems a little cruel that a man who, in a way, chronicled the last moments of so many maritime men, would be buried with so little fanfare of public recollection.

They played taps at the cemetery.

Nine people listened.

Since his death, the authors have reflected much on this man's life and works. Most of his unclaimed creations and personal effects were donated to the permanent art collection of Montcalm Community College, where Gary Hauck serves as Dean of Instruction. These pieces are currently on display in the "Ed Pusick Gallery" in the campus's Instruction North art building. Examples of his works and belongings housed there include two original color pencil drawings, original doodles, his humorous self-portrait, several well-known limited edition prints, photographs, his own artist's/drafting table, instruments, briefcase, and personal scrapbook memorabilia.

Reminiscent of a trip Lois took with Ed to deliver prints to the Whitefish Point Shipwreck Museum, Lois and Gary have together visited Michigan's Upper Peninsula to find a bronze marker the artist created, and to visit the sites of other Great Lakes disasters. The following chapters share his life story and works.

Lois Hauck sadly displays several of Ed Pusick's limited edition prints shortly after his funeral. (Photo courtesy of The Grand Rapids Press.)

Ed Pusick as a Young Man

Chapter 2

Ed's Life and Career
(Based on conversations with Lois Hauck)

Early Days

On a cold January 8th in 1927, Edward John Pusick came into the world. Born in a hospital (unusual at that time) in Battle Creek, Michigan, he was the son of John Charles Pusick and Bessie Belle Sampson Pusick. They were thrilled to have a healthy, baby boy.

The pediatric ward had a set schedule for when all the newborns were to be fed, but as Ed was later told by his mother, that "didn't suit hungry little Ed who awakened screaming from hunger. He was so loud that a nurse sneaked in and fed him extra to keep him quiet. Unfortunately, her actions were discovered and she was later fired!"

Ed stated of himself that he was a "wonderful baby," as long as his parents did what he wanted! But there was one thing he couldn't tolerate and that was a babysitter. When he grew a little older, one babysitter was even seen running from the house and heard screaming after he threw hot food on her. Only his Aunt Olive, Mother and maternal Grandmother were allowed by little Ed to watch him, or he threw a temper tantrum.

His brother David died of polio as a child. So, Ed was raised as an "only child" and spoiled by his parents, grandparents and extended family. With a childish scrawl at about age six, Ed wrote a note to his mother and David, "I love you Mother. You are 50. Full of love. Mother and David, too. David was pretty. He always wanted to kiss me."

He was raised in the Christian Science faith but later in life left that denomination for what he deemed "a more personal devotion." His mother allowed him to attend Sunday school just down the street and as he grew older he accepted "the more simple teachings of Christ instead."

Ed's Father

During his early years, Ed's father, John, was a plant manager with the title of Assistant Superintendent of a pumping station – the Union Steam Pump Company that made water and steam pumps during the Great Depression. The company was able to hire 800 men with two shifts and gave John the opportunity to work and provide for his family during a time when many were out of a job. This business is still in existence but has moved to Fort Custer near Battle Creek, and is now owned by a Japanese company.

Because of his position in this company, John was able to hire some good men. When his wife Bess told him of a friend whose husband had been out of work for quite a long time, John happily told her, "Bess, get her to send her husband down here and I'll give him a job."

John went on to study Mathematics at Valparaiso University in Indiana. He had cultivated math skills at age sixteen while working as an apprentice for a tool and dye company in Muskegon.

While still a junior at Valparaiso, he was invited to teach as a professor of math and mechanical engineering. His classes quickly became so popular that some filled with up to five hundred students! But evidently, the pay was minimal at best at the time and as a result he quit school before finishing.

At John's funeral on June 6, 1939, more than 6,000 people attended in a large auditorium in Battle Creek. Ed was only 12 years old. At the time of the funeral, he hadn't shed a tear and didn't until an event several weeks later.

His father had bought a new Ford only two months before his death. One day Ed and his mother were downtown near his father's plant and happened to be eating lunch at The Belmont Restaurant on Michigan Avenue. Their table was by the big bay window facing the street. Unknown to Ed, his mother had sold the car a few days earlier. Halfway through lunch Ed glanced up and with a startled look saw his dad's car pulling up to the stoplight. That's when it hit him that his dad wouldn't be coming back and he began sobbing almost uncontrollably.

Ed's Mother

Ed was always very close to his mother and during the latter days of her life, he became her chief caregiver. Among his belongings was a poem he sent to her:

"To a Mother"
In my heart entrusted strong
    I bear a love in solid will.
Of memory sweet and cherished long
    Remains unchanged but constant still.
And all my life and space of time
    I shall bear that love forevermore,
And dream the while of memories fine
    Of those past days and many more.
And when ere my righteous guardian calls
    And summons me to rest,
There in distant heavens halls
    We shall resume our love that was best.

Ed's Grandmother

Gertrude Sweeney was Ed's paternal grandmother. Born in Moscow, Russia, she was one of 18 children.

When she was only 5 years old she went to work at her parent's grocery store. This was a Czar-appointed business outside the Kremlin near the main gate and was only open to foreign tourists, diplomats and their families. Because of this early experience she became fluent in German, Russian, Italian, French, and Spanish and later became an interpreter for her parents along with the customers coming into the store.

At age 18 she immigrated to the United States, but somehow managed to bypass Ellis Island going directly to Chicago, using a Czar's grant to study at The University of Chicago.

Soon after coming to the U.S. she was heard saying, "I'm never going to be a baby machine like my mother!" Of course that was a reference to her 17 siblings!

Gertrude wasn't in college for very long because according to Ed's dad, "she was man crazy." She eventually became a chef and cooked for:

1. Charlie Chaplin – she cooked at his house and did many Hollywood parties for him. It was said that she liked to be in control and "bossed all of the other cooks at their parties."
2. Wallace Berry – he was an early silent-screen and later "talky" actor with a gravelly voice starring in *Tugboat Anny, 20 Mule-Team*, and other westerns before doing a later comedy with Jean Harlow.
3. Robert Taylor – She told the family that he wanted her to go to Mexico with him but she couldn't get away.
4. Clark Gable – He thought the world of her. She even showed Ed letters Gable had written her. He gave her a house located in the canyon at the top of the San Fernando Mountains. When Ed wanted to get in touch with his grandmother, he figured he could reach her by calling the president of the Screen Actors Guild. This man knew that Clark Gable would know where she was so he called Mr. Gable and he in turn told them where to reach Gertrude. Ed remembers visiting her and noticing how spry she was as she climbed up those steep hills.

Nothing was ever mentioned as to how Gertrude met her husband but she did get married and had two children, one being Ed's dad. Her husband later abandoned the family to become a priest. He went to Seminary and later died there.

Ed told the story about a tragic occurrence involving his grandmother that happened in Chicago after Gertrude's husband died. Gertrude and the family had been living in Chicago since her husband was from Illinois and Gertrude was working for The Western Electric Company. For their employees this business planned a huge picnic taking an excursion on a chartered boat across Lake Michigan to Michigan City, Indiana. Since 7,300 tickets were sold for the event they had to charter five passenger ships to accommodate everyone, one of the ships being the Eastland, the boat that Gertrude was on.

Estimates showed that more than 2,500 people had boarded without the crew being very attentive to overloading. Before departure (at the Clark Street dock in Chicago) the ship capsized to one side and threw many of the passengers into the Chicago River! Ed's grandmother did survive but she was one of the fortunate ones since most were trapped in cabins below. July 24, 1915 will go down in history as being the worst Great Lakes area shipwreck with 835 people losing their lives (*Shipwreck Journal*, Spring 1998: 3).

Ed remembers this grandmother coming to Battle Creek twice to visit. The first time she brought Ed's cousin Eugene, named after Ed's uncle on his dad's side. Eugene was two years younger than Ed and having never seen coal before, he became fascinated with their "Michigan cellar." They spent a good many hours playing down there and getting dirty like little boys do.

When Ed was only eight years old he remembers this grandmother coming for another visit. She didn't like Ed's mother and the feeling was mutual. She was going to "kidnap" her grandson and take him back with her to California because she claimed Ed's mother was an unfit parent and wife. She had noticed that his mother let him come in at all hours of the night, covered with mud from head to foot and having no curfew whatsoever. One evening Ed was still gone even though it was

11

getting dark. Gertrude asked his mother where he was and she replied, "He will come home when he's hungry."

One of Ed's writings illustrates this "freedom" at a young age:

On hot summer days, during the 30's it was my habit to seek pleasant relief from the heat in the cooling atmosphere of the water park, and I was usually clad in a heavy cotton/ wool bathing suit. Swim trunks had yet to be invented, and air conditioning in those days was a new fad introduced in a few movie theaters.

Comprising about half an acre, the subject water park lies in a flat depression well below the level of 17 Forest Street where I once lived. The brook with no name runs through it, although in a wide half-circle, easterly direction until changing to a northerly course; the stream being traversable in three places via small foot bridges. At the time, the footing in this locale was firm and solid throughout, yet featuring several unique physical terrain properties.

At its northern end, a rusty pipe of about an inch and a half in diameter protruded from a lid-covered, small artisan well; its clear, icy cold water draining directly over the brook.

Elsewhere, in the park's center, there existed a pool of clear spring water, its borders confined with a cemented enclosure measuring, roughly, 15 feet long by 10 feet wide. This pond, with a depth of three or so feet, revealed a black muck bottom without vegetation of any kind; yet, amazingly, there were always minnows in the water and, at times, several small brook trout; the same species of fish which inhabited the park's running stream.

South of the railroad embankment where the brook entered the park from its large iron conduit, lay the main attraction for neighborhood children. The brook, issuing with force from the pipe or conduit under the railroad (over the years) scoured a 20 foot long post with a mean depth of three feet.

It was there I spent many happy hours, sometimes with other kids, playing with toy boats, one being a spring-propeller powered miniature submarine which would actually submerge for awhile and then resurface. Occasionally, though, (on a dare!) I would cross under the railroad embankment via the pipe; or otherwise, bathe in the icy cold water until near death from hyperthermia.

Upon reaching home, my mother became accustomed to seeing my ghostly pallor with blue lips. Her only complaint, though, applied to my mud covered condition; that, and the sand in my swim suit, the latter being something which never failed to provoke my mother's anger. This would occur whenever she caught me changing my swim suit for street clothes—inside the house. I disliked to hose off, outdoors, with the garden hose. My usual argument was that its water was too cold. (Handwritten)

One day Ed and his mother were visiting Ed's other grandmother (maternal). Gertrude, the overbearing grandmother from California came over angrily sending Ed's mother fleeing while Ed and the other grandmother barricaded themselves upstairs in the bedroom. With determination in her eyes and furry written all over her face, Gertrude stomped up the stairs. She pounded on the door then threw all of her weight against it, demanding, "Let me in right now!" They held their breath hoping the lock would hold!

She yelled that she would get a private detective to take Ed to her home in California. Ed's dad finally came in and tried to calm her down. Actually he didn't like her either and thought she was an old busybody. Wanting her to return to California immediately, he personally drove her to the train station in Kalamazoo with Ed in the back seat.

Early Life in School

When Ed was in first grade he had the opportunity to meet Dr. William K. Kellogg (founder of the Kellogg [Cereal] Company), who came to visit his class. Mr. Kellogg brought in a calf's liver that was frozen in dry ice, planning to use it as an object lesson. Pulling out a large mallet, he lifted it over his head; bringing the mallet down on the calves liver and smashing it into pieces he said, "Your liver will be like this if you drink alcohol!" Ed is convinced this image must have stayed in many of these young minds even when they got older!

When Ed was 10 years old, Ed's dad let him drive the car from Battle Creek to Traverse City. Traveling up Route 31 they passed some huge sand dunes with Ed exclaiming, "Oh boy! I didn't know we had mountains in Michigan!" This was after they had passed an 800 foot dune that was two miles long replete with trees.

Ed sheepishly relayed a sad story that happened to him while in grade school. He would have been around 10 or 11 years old. The badgering started almost as soon as Ed stepped foot into the school yard on this particular day. He was taunted and ridiculed about being the "teacher's pet" with an "oversized bully" threatening to beat him up the following day. Ed remembers running home and telling his mother. Her response was that he would just have to "take care of it" himself.

Several days passed with each one ending the same way, Ed being chased through the woods with the bully yelling taunts. And each day Ed made it home just in time to safety since he could outrun this hoodlum.

While at the library one day, he stumbled across an old Indian folklore book. In this tattered volume he found a chapter that graphically depicted how to make a trap. Without thinking of how this contraption could cause serious injuries, or the outcome of any such endeavor, he began constructing a device that would "punish" this pest.

The bully always chased him past a dump that had several old discarded refrigerators, ancient rusty lawnmowers, and rickety chairs. Ed decided that the trap would be built in this area and began digging a ditch on the path leading past the dump. This trench was just around a bend in the path so one wouldn't be able to see it until the last moment when it would be too late.

Each day after running home from being chased, Ed backtracked and returned to this spot to dig until the hole was wide and deep enough. Next, he worked on "planting" various "weapons" down in the trench-like trap! These implements were constructed earlier from pieces of old disposed dumpster items and were strategically placed down in the hole. (One wouldn't think that a 10-year old boy could devise such a plan as this!)

During this week, Ed "led" the troublemaker along a different path while being chased home, not wanting the bully to know what was about to befall him.

Finally his trap was finished! Ed made some trial runs to test his skills in hurtling over the trench. He most definitely would have to clear it while being chased! The next day would be the day to try it out!

Again, the bully, yelling that he would beat him up as soon as he caught up to him, started chasing him home. With a gleam on his face Ed turned down the path that led past the dump but coming upon the trench he jumped and cleared the area. The boy, not far behind, didn't see the hole until it was too late and down he went. As Ed kept running he heard screaming like he had never known before but kept going until he reached home.

This bully wasn't in school the next day, or the next. At the end of the week his teacher said, "Class I have some very sad news to share with you. George won't be coming back to class because he was involved in a terrible accident and the doctors weren't able to help after infection set in. I think it would be a good idea to take up a collection to give his mother to help cover the cost of his funeral."

"Oh what have I done!? What have I done!?" Ed moaned to himself. "I didn't mean to hurt him in that way! I only wanted to teach him a lesson!" Feeling very wretched, Ed couldn't concentrate on his classwork or do anything else the rest of the day. His mind kept going to the gruesome discovery of George's lifeless body, and the vision that maybe he had been able to crawl home leaving a trail of blood after having been impaled on the primitive contraption.

To somewhat appease his conscience Ed became one of the chief contributors to the funeral fund. Ed used all the money he had saved from his allowance to help the family out. No one ever found out his other "contribution" or involvement in the accident but it haunted him the rest of his days. It served as a reminder to try to curb this "mean streak" that he had when provoked and not take matters into his own hands. At least, this is the story Ed shared.

High School and Young Romance

During his high school days, Ed enjoyed some level of popularity, and even starred in some schools plays and musical productions. He had a huge crush on a beautiful majorette. He stared at her so much that his teacher, Phil Johnson (who had also been Ernest Hemingway's teacher) decided to make Ed move up near his teaching desk. Ed never went out with her but continued to be enamored by her beauty and thought about her through years to come.

Mr. Johnson thought that Ed's essays were to be compared to those of Ernest Hemingway and told him so. But he didn't want Ed to copy Ernest's behavior. According to Johnson, "Back in the day Ernest terrorized the girls and even brought snakes to class one day! Another day he tied their pigtails together, dipped them in the inkwells and later brought a gunny sack full of live creatures that were squirming all over the place. When he emptied the bag in front of the girls, there were several squirrels with their tails tied together!" Mr. Johnson remarked, "Ed, I know you'd never do any of these things!" (Of course, he had no idea of the tragic episode during Ed's grade school days!)

In the meantime Ed had his eyes on another gorgeous girl. Soon he and Gloria were seeing a lot of each other. They often went to her house where Ed also enjoyed being with her parents.

Even when he joined the Navy immediately after graduation, he and Gloria still corresponded. During his initial leave the first thing he wanted to do was go to her house, where she still lived with her parents. He sent word that he'd be there at a certain time. When he arrived there was no one at home. Her parents were at work since they both were baggage handlers at the train depot. So down to the train station he went with questions as to where she could be. To his utter shock and dismay he found out a deep dark secret. They said, "Ed, we guess it's time you should know this but during the period you were dating our daughter was already married to a sailor!"

Of course Ed was crushed and it took quite a while to get over that kind of news! Many years later while working at Gage Printing, his secretary came in to say there was a beautiful young woman waiting to see him. Emerging from his office and full of curiosity, Ed discovered Gloria standing there much to his surprise! She was now a divorcee and decided she wanted to pick up where they had left off! But Ed wasn't interested in starting another relationship with her and told her so.

Periodically he stayed in town after work to have dinner at a private club on the third floor on "Bank Corners." (During the Depression there was a bank on three corners.) Ed was drinking his second bottle of beer and eating peanuts before ordering dinner when in walked a tall, gorgeous brunette with a very nice figure. She was accompanied by two male business acquaintances but that didn't stop her from doing a little flirting with Ed. He later discovered from one of her friends that her name was Nancy and she was the head of the Michigan Republican Committee and living on a grant, not making much money.

On many occasions one could find the two of them chatting together at a private nightclub and it wasn't long before Nancy invited Ed to come home with her. Since neither of them owned a car, they took a cab that soon pulled up in front of a spectacular mansion near the sanitarium on Champion Street. "Here we are," said Nancy as Ed's eyes opened wide. She quickly corrected his assumption and explained that the house was not hers, but the W. K. Kellogg house where she roomed and boarded!

Nancy reached in her purse pulling out a set of keys to unlock the gated wall surrounding the sprawling estate. When they reached the door, she rang the bell to summon the maid. A prim woman in a black uniform with a white lacy cap came to greet them and led them down a long corridor. Carved black ebony wainscoting lined the left side of the hall. The right side had rose marble adorned with many original oil paintings, including what looked like a Rembrandt. The hallway appeared to recede for as far back as one could see.

With some authority Nancy told the maid, "Bring in some snacks." Then she added, "Is the fire still going?" As she turned to open some double framed doors a large, warm fire roaring in the fireplace was revealed. The setting was perfect for a romantic rendezvous! (Ed was drawing a picture of this house and room as he was relaying this story.) They sat down on the luxurious cream colored sofa, maybe just a little too close, then … she started talking politics! Later that evening she exclaimed, "You sure are interesting!"

On their second date, just when he thought she was "coming on to him" she emphatically stated, "Isn't politics fascinating?" What a letdown! Ed was puzzled how he had become involved with someone who could talk of nothing else.

Not long after this, Nancy said she had something important to ask him and proceeded to request that he accompany her to her chalet in Switzerland.

While that might have sounded romantic, Ed decided he didn't like how she was handling their "romance." Besides, he really preferred to "pursue but not be pursued." He stopped going to the club in case he might run into her again.

After "jilting" Nancy, Ed became involved with the local civic theater. (He had an interest in theater since the days in which he played the lead male role in the 1943 production of "Ever Since Eve" at the Battle Creek Senior High School.) A friend of his who was employed at Consumers Energy taught him how to work the sets and do the lighting. He became acquainted with Mrs. Mildred Genebach, wife of the owner and founder of United Steel and Wire Company, the first company to make shopping carts. She had become involved with the theater and began teaching Ed how to work behind the scenes.

After rehearsals Ed went with the whole gang to a favorite hangout on the west side called The Hotel Heart. Many dignitaries, mostly ladies, hung out there. But while Ed was looking around admiring "the view" he began telling his friends about Nancy and how she not only came on to him but was rather strange in how she did it. Mrs. Genebach exclaimed, "Oh Ed! You big fool! With your feeble mind didn't you realize who that young woman was that you 'let go?' She was heiress to the whole Kellogg fortune!" The look on Ed's face was priceless as the others laughed at his dismay.

Service in the Navy

Ed enlisted in the United States Navy seven months before he graduated from High School. This was no surprise to his family since his mother's lineage traced back to seafarers and New England ship captains, including a U.S. Navy admiral. Even his paternal uncle, a former commander in the U.S. Navy, was a skipper on a large ocean freighter.

Though having missed graduation, special arrangements were made by Ed's principal, who considered him to be one of their most outstanding students. To Ed's surprise and delight his diploma arrived on his ship!

Later he wrote:

Scholastically speaking—and for reasons too lengthy to explain here—I was a semester ahead of my classmates in many subjects. For that reason in 1943, I attended school only in the mornings. The principal, Bystron, secured a part-time position for me in the Battle Creek City Engineering Department working afternoons as a file clerk, apprentice draftsman and surveyor's assistant.

By the autumn of '44, I had earned sufficient school credits to graduate the following year, so I enlisted in the Navy and it wasn't long before I found myself aboard a ship bound for the North Polar Region along with Murmansk, Russia.

Shortly after these events, Ed had the opportunity to get in touch with his Aunt Evelyn for the first time -- his paternal grandmother Gertrude's daughter, and half-sister to Ed's dad. He recounted:

In the spring of 1946 while on leave from a ship anchored in the San Francisco Bay I had the opportunity to visit Los Angeles and to call Aunt Evelyn at her Hollywood, California residence. I had sourced the phone number from her mother (Gertrude Sweeney) who told me her daughter was the wife of one of the Warner Brothers, most notably the famous movie magnate, producer.

I vividly remember Evelyn's displeasure upon receiving my call. She promptly hung up on me!

My father, who met Evelyn when she was a teenager, once said that although she had great beauty, she also had a mean disposition! (Personal conversation)

After World War II, Ed was in Marsailles, France. On a clear, cloudless day, after being given liberty, he left the ship wearing his dress blues. Marsailles was a city that had very little damage from the war with the exception of a blown up bridge. Busses lined up near the ship to take the sailors into town. On the way they passed a carnival then continued on only to slow down beside of a large warehouse where G.I.'s had crowded around. People were shouting, "Free beer in cans!" They saw Ed and motioned for him to come in. He didn't hesitate and not only went in but was treated like a hero.

Afterwards he went to a movie theater that showed films with English subtitles. It was late afternoon when the movie started and he soon lost track of time. When he emerged from the theater it was past curfew and the streets were deserted! He had missed his bus back to the ship which was about 25-30 miles away! He stopped by a bar that was still open but no one could understand him. Not even the M.P.'s were out to help him.

He encountered a young sailor dressed in his whites who had also missed the bus. Soon a G.I. driving a truck came along but said he could only take them to the outskirts of town because he was already late to report to his depot. "Maybe you'll be lucky and another G.I. will come along," he offered.

They were dropped off near a 1200-foot mountain. Signs were posted in French and German but he could only make out the words *Auch Tun* ("Attention"). Barbed wire had been put there at the beginning of the war by the Germans.

Ed thought that if they climbed the mountain it would cut off some miles and on the top they would be able to see the glow from the ships lights. He knew his ship was to leave by 7:00 the next morning so it was crucial that he get there before they set sail.

The two sailors took turns lifting the barbed wire beneath these signs so that each could climb through. The terrain was rugged and the higher they climbed the more their ears began popping. Before they got to the top they reached an area that once had been a cave but now a grotto had been constructed with a concrete slab on top. They noticed remnants of hundreds of candles and rosaries piled here and there, evidence that people had once come to pray. They figured it must have been a shrine at one time before the war began.

Just then the moon's rays broke through the clouds and shone down on the concrete slab illuminating an inscription stating that St. Frances of Assisi had suffered his "Stigmata" in the 15th century at that very spot! It was believed to be "an act of God." According to the inscription, another man had witnessed this happening to St. Frances where his hands, feet, and side were pierced. After this phenomenon St. Frances retreated back into this cave and died. It was reported that before he died, St. Frances knelt before a crucifix that was at the entrance, and uttered, "Let me suffer for Thy sake."

After seeing this shrine and being utterly amazed that they had literally stumbled upon it, the two sailors continued to the top where Ed was relieved to see his illuminated ship below. The other sailor was from a much smaller ship and couldn't seem to see it. Ed told him he could get help from the M.P.'s when they arrived below and they began their descent.

Halfway down they could see a big commotion in front of a large building surrounded by barbed wire at the base of the mountain. M.P.'s were running out carrying their weapons as their gaze was riveted to the sight of two lone figures descending from the mountain in the moonlight. Several officers, one being a Lt. Colonel, also came out to view what was going on.

When Ed reached the fence he could hear them shouting (after they recovered from their astonishment!) They were saying it must be a miracle that these two sailors crossed the mountain unharmed because it was an un-cleared German minefield! There had been others blown up in the past just stepping near it! Those viewing Ed and his friend coming down the mountain had been watching in suspense just waiting for something to happen. Ed and this friend had somehow missed the English signs that had been posted warning of the danger.

Ed managed to reach his ship just as it was about to sail. He truly believed that the spirit of St. Frances of Assisi had saved his life!

Between Wars

After WWII Ed worked for the Electric Boat Company in Groton, Connecticut, and later decided to become a student of architecture at the Midwestern Technical Institute in Chicago. One day while reading the Chicago Tribune he noticed a photo that would later become known as "The Lost View of the Cathedral Rheims" (Belgium). This gorgeous Cathedral had been blown to smithereens during WWI but up until this point there were no photos in existence showing what it looked like before the destruction.

Ed took the photo and began a large charcoal rendering of the subject. Upon completion, his teacher who studied under Frank Lloyd Wright put some of his own finishing touches to the project and commended Ed on a job well done.

The director of the Institute was Russian. He had befriended Ed and on many occasions, even picked him up to take him places in his car. One day this director decided to go back to Russia and turned in his resignation. Ed decided to give his drawing to this man as a going away gift.

Ed forgot about the picture rendering until one day walking down Michigan Avenue he happened to spot it in the window where an auction was occurring! Upon entering the premises he was immediately escorted out because the dress attire was formal and he was in casual clothes. Unfortunately he had failed to sign the drawing so there was a card underneath stating: "Artist Unknown."

Not too long afterwards he happened to pass a six-story billboard near the river advertising for Prudential Life Insurance. In the corner of this sign was his drawing as their new insignia! They continued using this logo for years on all of their policies!

In a letter dated to Lois on November 6, 2003 Ed wrote:

> Yesterday, after you left, I decided to take a nap. Then, whilst in my bed—with frontal lobes relaxed—the name of that famous Czech composer (I had been trying to recall for you) came to mind. It was Anton Dvorak, 1841-1904; and Dvorak is pronounced "(da-) 'vor - zhak," in case you didn't know.
>
> Anyhow, Dvorak orchestrated "Pictures of an exhibition" and composed what is considered to be the world's greatest cello concerto; also, while touring some of our nation's western states, he composed "The New World Symphony." I am confident you are familiar with its melodic themes. And were Dvorak alive today, I would request that he compose a symphony to commemorate my charcoal study: *Lost View of the Cathedral Rheims*. Had it been officially recognized as my work, though, can you imagine the residuals I might have received from it? (Handwritten)

Ed eventually found a job with Gage Printing in Battle Creek as a nameplate decal artist and designer. Howard Hughes saw some of Ed's work and requested through his boss that Ed do a "secret" project for him. He was given instructions as to what Mr. Hughes wanted so he began working on this large and seemingly important undertaking. Years later Ed wrote a note saying:

> I found the Gage Co. catalog which gives a photocopy view of the airfoil section of a jet blade that Howard Hughes

requested be deep-etched on a precision plastic comparator chart of enormous size, and that I be the draftsman. However, once the chart was made, no one could figure out how the strange looking device was to be used, or what the blade was for. (Handwritten)

Ed recalls that when the project was finished his boss contacted Howard Hughes who made odd arrangements to meet him in Nevada. His boss was to take a specific train that was to let him out "in the desert" and there Mr. Hughes would be waiting for him. Ed never got paid for doing this assignment and whatever Mr. Hughes paid was given to his boss.

Recalled to Active Duty

Because he was recalled to active duty as a reservist at the beginning of the Korean War, more than 25 years passed before Ed took up artwork again.

It was 1950 when Ed was assigned to LST 306. This Landing Ship Tank was taken out of mothballs from WW2. The compartments had been sealed and covered to preserve them from rust although the ship was still in water. A lot of painting, scraping and polishing had to be done. This work gave Ed a whole new view of the phrase, "getting it into ship shape."

Ed was assigned as a quarter master learner where his duties were in the wheelhouse being in charge of the charts and navigation apparatus. He also had to monitor the radios that were in the wheelhouse.

By this time Ed was an experienced seaman, but a total novice was selected to captain the LST 306. Having seen service in World War II, Captain Pearce was assigned to this LST; however, he never had any prior sea time! The only experience he had was that he had been a professor! This was not exactly a qualification to captain a ship and Ed was appalled that someone without the right training had been chosen for this task! But the assignment proved uneventful and life at sea went on.

One day the ship headed downstream in the beautiful St. Johns River in Florida. Depths were 10 feet and the water was clear enough to see the bottom. On his chart Ed could see that they were coming up to an ancient pirate's shipwreck. He not only could see some of the remains of the ship but the pristine waters gave glimpse of perfectly preserved timbers. He would have liked to linger in that area at least long enough to examine everything that was visible. How often does one get to see a wrecked pirate ship?

They made their way towards Jacksonville but because of scores of other Navy vessels in the Navy Yard there was no berthing, or safe distance from the other ships. They had to wait upstream and found a place to drop anchor. St. Augustine and Jacksonville were both equidistant from the ship (25 miles). The open stern was jutting out into a very narrow point of the St. John River. There they remained at anchor for several days.

On one of these idle days Ed went out on the stern to have a smoke. Several dark blue, male bottle-nosed dolphins made their way over and began making a noise. Ed started to mimic them and when he did this they stood up on their tails! The next day this same scene was repeated and again they performed to Ed's delight. By then some of the females were in the area with their cows (babies). Ed reached into his pocket for a can of sardines to feed them. Since the adult dolphins quickly gobbled these up he went back inside to scour around and found two more cans.

He observed that the males swam in the area first since they were the guardians. They cleared the route to scare off the sharks. When they deemed it was safe, the females and babies came along. Ed was enraptured, so much so, that his mind began working overtime. This was the beginning of how he became the pioneer of using dolphins for wartime activities.

He got the idea that they could be used by the Navy for spy missions, carrying messages underwater. He also figured out how they could be used to attach depth charges on the hulls of enemy ships. These would be magnetic bombs that would blow the ship up! When he approached the Navy about his idea they actually took him seriously and had him type up his thoughts to send to the University of Florida in Tallahassee. Navy intelligence quickly adopted this ingenious method.

His interest in dolphins never waned from that point on. Delightedly he accepted an assignment, at the age of 23, to help train dolphins for military use. There were four being used for this special training, Buddy, Minnea, Katie and Gracie, and he took charge of putting two of these through certain drills. Someone else was instructing the other two.

He swam with them to teach one of the female dolphins to use her flat nose to plant metal magnets on an old ship. Another dolphin followed, planting the explosive device on this magnet then quickly swimming off. Ed not only changed the distance each time but he also had to keep track of the time it took for each drill.

It was Ed's understanding that the Navy was still using this particular method at the time he was relaying this story in 2005. Several people have since verified this claim saying they had been to Bermuda recently and the tour guide explained how the dolphins in the area had been released from being used in the military.

Several times his ship stopped in Jamaica. He became fascinated with the area and loved when they returned. Even later in life, he returned to vacation there on several occasions.

Being an expert swimmer he spent many hours at the beach whenever he could. With a smile from ear-to-ear, he recalled the day he got to swim with Bo Derek! Of course this was before she became a well-known movie star. The two of them swam out past the reef while her husband, who was an older man, sat in a chair on the beach watching them. She was more brazen than he was and swam even further than he thought would be safe. (He described her provocative bathing suit in great detail.)

Meeting Captain McSorley

It was 1951 and Ed was 24 years old. One day his ship came down the river to Jacksonville, passing under a bridge and docking by the Merchant Marine/U.S. Navy Shipyard, east of the bridge. A fleet of Liberty ships was being re-commissioned and one in particular, belonging to the Merchant Marines, was having the hull scraped and painted.

A sailor from this old ship came over to Ed and told him he had heard that they had supplies of sugar, coffee beans, cream and other pantry items. Knowing how lousy the coffee was on his own ship, Ed arranged a trade with this sailor. In exchange they received coffee and delicious roast beef sandwiches.

One day it was Ed's turn to carry the supplies to this ship that was being repainted. As Ed was walking the gangplank, he noticed that on the deck was a burly watchman leaning back in a chair. The large figure was dressed in dungarees and had no cap to cover his short cropped hair, exposing his weather beaten and tough-looking face. He greeted Ed and took him back to fix him some freshly brewed coffee and a roast beef sandwich. That's when Ed noticed that the kitchen had a restaurant percolator. No wonder their coffee was good. Crewmen on his ship just boiled coffee grounds and served it grounds and all

This watchman asked, "Would you like a tour?" Of course Ed thought that would be great. The watchman took Ed back on deck where a welder was working. The welder looked up, saluted and said to this watchman, "Hello Captain!" As Ed recovered from shock he stuttered, "Ca-ca Captain???" The captain smiled, put out his hand and said, "Captain Ernest M. McSorley."

He told Ed that he was only there temporarily and was waiting to be commissioned on one of the Great Lakes ore boats. This assignment would end up making him the youngest Master of a merchant vessel on the Great Lakes! (McSorley ended up serving as a seasoned captain for 40 years, being more known as the last captain of the *Edmund Fitzgerald* 1972-1975!)

Ed told the captain of his own aspirations of becoming a merchant sailor. "Don't do it!" the captain exclaimed. "It's a tough life and you'll be with bad men, some of which are criminals. You'll wind up on deck and have to work your way up through the ranks. The only way is to go to college first to be an officer."

Ed was so disappointed to hear this news because he had for a long time wanted to continue on in the military. At the age of 24 he considered himself to be an experienced seaman but had to admit that this seasoned captain would know what he was talking about.

At the base of the large bridge at the old shipyard in Jacksonville stands a black, bronze monument of a sailor leaning forward and manning a ship's wheel. Later, those who knew Ed claimed that he bore a strong resemblance to this figure. It may very well be Ed, for on the second of two trips to Norfolk from Jacksonville he received a permanent disability. As the ship was leaving Norfolk, it encountered a terrific storm with forty-to-fifty-foot waves. If it hadn't been for Ed's expertise the ship would have gone down. He was later publically commended for his bravery but it was during this storm that Ed suffered an injury to his leg as he was thrown off of a ladder. When the storm subsided and they were awaiting an ambulance to take Ed to the hospital, he remembered hearing the Captain tell him to "hurry back," but he was never able to return to service.

Early Drawings

Ed was fired in the spring of 1976 from "the only job [he] ever loved." He had been working since 1971 as a boss of the western division of a large security firm in Grand Rapids that put in 6,000 man-hours weekly. He wasn't sure what happened to cause the termination except there were some people in his department who decided he needed to go if they wanted to move up. Ed felt that his personal high standards for excellence and safety cost him his job.

Turning to his more artistic abilities, Ed began to draw sketches, produce watercolor paintings, and create color pastels. (His mother had been a talented watercolorist and portraitist, and he had already discovered his own inborn artistic ability.) In an effort to freelance as an illustrator, he compiled a professional-looking portfolio with 40 large pages of his works. He titled it, "A Portfolio of Renderings by: E. Pusick." True to his humorous bent, the first page depicted a splashed drop of water using white pastel on black paper. The caption read, "This is only a drop in the bucket." The portfolio included samples of sketch ideas for decorative decals, wall decorations, catalogs, advertisements, fashions, and architectural illustrations. Full-color examples featured butterflies, flowers, stained-glass windows, fish, antique cars, boats, home interiors and exteriors, farms, trains, furniture, lamps, and human figures.

It was this portfolio that landed him a job as an independent contractor in Kentwood, Michigan working for a small church-design firm that was originally called "First Design" then "Brady Barnes & Neal." The beautiful studio was situated in open land, which is now at the end of one of the runways of the Gerald R. Ford Airport in Grand Rapids. Sometimes deer came up and peered into the window while Ed was busy drawing. While there he received training as an architectural delineator. That's when he began using pastels as his preferred medium.

This firm specialized in building churches not only in town but out of state. Ed's color pastel drawings were a more practical way to show the client how the finished structure would look. Ed put his trademark in the corner of every one and at the time it wasn't his signature or initials but a tiny drawing of a wild rabbit.

One of the firm's architects, Mike McFarlin, soon befriended Ed. He recognized Ed's abilities and enjoyed interacting with him even though their shifts barely overlapped. (Ed reported at 4 pm, which was nearly the end of the work day for the other six to eight members of the staff, and spent the quiet evening hours illustrating the church blueprints that had just been drafted.)

Ed became fascinated with an old book that he had on WWI plane fights. A number of evenings he came to work but found there was nothing to do. So he "fooled around," sketching aerial dogfights while his favorite classical music played in the background on his old record player. He finished his sketch that he modestly called a doodle, and left if on the drawing board as he went home for the night.

McPharlin saw the drawing the next day and asked Ed, "Why are you wasting your talents on these aerial drawings? Have you ever considered illustrating shipwrecks of the Great Lakes?" Until this point Ed had no interest in doing so. Besides, the only one he knew about was the one that his grandmother almost perished on, *The Eastland*. "You would be good at not only illustrating these ships but doing so in the act of sinking." Mike, being a "Great Lakes maritime history buff who believed Ed's creative skills should be applied to its many interesting vessel subjects," told Ed about his copies of Fred Stonehouse's books on shipwrecks (Tom Farnquist, Spring 1992, p.4). He encouraged Ed to read them the first chance he got. Ed rolled his eyes but to appease him said, "Bring them in and I'll look at them sometime." One of Ed's own writings reveals that as a boy growing up, he didn't know much about the Great Lakes or their importance in maritime history (see Chapter 4).

One night Ed came to work and there didn't seem to be anything to do. The stormy evening seemed to put him "in the mood" for reading Stonehouse's books on shipwrecks. The more violent the storm got, the more Ed read. He was hooked! Inspired! He felt compelled to begin his first shipwreck drawing and with a driving force he worked until he completed his "Magnificent Obsession." He didn't rest until it was done. It wasn't enjoyable but he knew he had to do it (McPharlin).

His beginning pastels were crude. He was just a learner. He couldn't seem to get the wave action but the following year in the spring he happened to stumble upon a PBS special that gave him an idea. This documentary featured the story of a Venetian artist who lived around the year 1450. Something clicked in Ed's mind when he saw a certain procedure this Florentine used to draw the violent action of water. He decided to copy this technique and later perfected it so much that he claimed he would take his "secret" method to his grave.

Ed's first attempt at using this unusual technique was *The Last Voyage of the Edmund Fitzgerald*. Not being able to take his eyes off of it, Mike asked if he could have it. Ed gladly gave it to him since he didn't like it at all.

His boss called the local TV station to tell the station about Ed's particular talent. In the fall of '77 Ed was interviewed by a reporter who took pictures of his works to show on TV. By then Ed was working to make improvements on his illustrations of shipwrecks, still giving away all of his originals, being superstitious that it wasn't right to "profit from the dead." He gave what he claimed to be one of his best to the bookkeeper from his firm. The work was a tranquil scene of an old wreck on a beach. Unfortunately this bookkeeper was later arrested for doctoring the books so whatever became of this drawing, no one knows.

Finally Ed succeeded in finishing what he considered his masterpiece: *Wreck on South Fox Island*. It was around this time that Fred Stonehouse and his wife came to town to meet Ed at his studio and take him out for dinner. Fred thought that pastel renderings were an impractical method for promoting the mystery of the Great Lakes shipwrecks so he gave Ed the idea to do his works in black and white. Fred convinced him that color was too expensive and black and white drawings were easier to replicate. He gave him many books and research materials along with several extremely rare photo glossies of ill-fated vessels. He also suggested that Ed could get some good publicity if he donated his drawings to museums and libraries. That appealed to Ed since he was already giving his works away.

Ed did switch to pencil renderings which resulted in a more dramatic form depicting the horror of "going down." The success of his method of "doodling" with the pencil medium of expression led to Ed's introduction to Tom Farnquist, Executive Director of the Great Lakes Shipwreck Historical Society. "This very talented maritime illustrator with his fine skillful insight and experience has produced works for the Society which have helped us in our presentation and interpretation of maritime history" (Tom Farnquist, Spring '92, p.7).

To his delight Ed was invited to go along on an expedition in 1989 to explore the waters of Lake Superior, seventeen miles off the coast of Whitefish Point in Canadian waters. This was where the wreckage of the *Edmund Fitzgerald* had been found. The Michigan Sea Grant program organized this three-day dive to survey the *Fitzgerald* with the primary objective being to do a 3-D video recording for use in museum educational programs and productions of documentaries. Participants included the National Oceanic and Atmospheric Administration (NOAA), The United States Army Corps of Engineers, the Great Lakes

Shipwreck Historical Society (GLSHS), the United States Fish and Wildlife Service, and the National Geographic Society.

The GLSHS used part of the five hours of video footage produced during these dives in a documentary and the National Geographic Society used a segment in a broadcast. Ed capitalized on this experience to produce probably one of his most widely-known works entitled, *Don't Allow Nobody on Deck!* which reportedly was the off-microphone order of Captain Ernest McSorley to his crew during the late afternoon on November 10, 1975. The admonition was overheard by the pilot of another vessel in radio contact with the *Edmund Fitzgerald*.

In 1999, the History Channel incorporated two of Ed's drawings, *They Lost the Struggle* and *Don't Allow Nobody on Deck!* They were included in an episode of The History Channel's series "Wrath of God" tentatively entitled, "Shipwrecks on the Great Lakes." (A 2005 commemorative edition print of *Don't Allow Nobody on Deck!* became one of Ed's most famous works.)

EDWARD PUSICK

A ZKA SPECIAL LIMITED EDITION COMMEMORATIVE PRINT

"Don't allow nobody on deck!"

- Reportedly, the off-mike order of Captain Ernest McSorley
to his crew during the late afternoon of November 10, 1975.
The admonition was overheard by the pilot of another
vessel in radio contact with the Edmund Fitzgerald.

Ed and Lois had the privilege of meeting Captain Fredrick Leete III in 2005. This seasoned seaman and one of the two divers who obtained the bell off of the *Edmund Fitzgerald*, had contacted Ed earlier in the year saying that he had just seen a poor copy of *The Edmund Fitzgerald in Storm,* an earlier companion drawing to *Don't Allow Nobody on Deck!* Leete's wish was that he could purchase a clearer one. They became "pen pals" and corresponded frequently.

The following letter dated July 24, 2004 explained that Ed had a special copy to give to Capt. Leete:

Ahoy there, Captain Leete:

It was an extraordinary find! While preparing a large collection of recently discovered (rare) limited edition prints to send to the Great Lakes Shipwreck Historical Society, I discovered a print of the "Edmund Fitzgerald in Storm," the one you previously sought.

The print bears my signature and it's dated 4.28.83; yet it seems that due to a large number of tiny water spots, I withheld it from circulation. Even so, these flaws are not discernible unless the print is held against a strong light source; therefore, I'm happy to announce the last "Fitz" image should make its upbound trip to you, sir, in the immediate future. And, as always no payment is acceptable for my work.

Both of us hope to rendezvous with you at Mackinaw City on, or about, the 25th of August.

Now, then: "Set all the special sea detail"
Anchors Aweigh
Ed
(Handwritten)

Then again before the trip he wrote another:

Dear Captain:

Thank you for your gracious letter of July 27, including

the excellent (map) directions to your "Wenniway" cottage. However, Lois and I plan to visit you during our downbound trip, Aug. 25, from the U.P. Even so, my concern is that you are on the mend and able to see us.

My maritime illustration endeavors ended 15 years ago, and during the interim, I lost 80-85 percent of my eyesight! But thanks to modern, state of the art surgical techniques, I now wear artificial eye implants; altogether superior to the vision I was born with. But lacking the skill, patience and interest I once had, those illustrations now—and I take liberty in saying this—"belong to the ages!"

Whenever there's time—and I haven't seen much of that—I pursue creative writing, with two book manuscripts awaiting completion … perhaps, a year from now. One of them details a prolonged mutiny at sea, a revolt the U.S. Navy has yet to go public with. The, often, violent mutiny occurred aboard a large troop transport ship where I saw duty as a deck-force seaman; and when many of the mutineers attempted to take my life (using homemade knives), the rapid response of an (O.D.) officer-on-deck, Lt. Dibrell, brought armed U.S. Marines to the rescue. But for that, my grave would be located in some military cemetery.

The last, rare, print of "The Edmund Fitzgerald in Storm" will be hand carried to you, sir; and we shall do our best to ensure it's safe arrival, assuming, of course, I can reach you.

Being unable to raise either foot higher than four inches, negotiating steps or street curbs is an impossible task, unless I'm descending them. In view of that, we might be obliged to hold our auspicious meeting at a quick serve, local eatery. Hamburgers with fries make a delicious repast for Lois and me.

C'est la vie,'
(so it goes)
Ed
(Handwritten)

"The Executive Suite" -- Ed's "Self Portrait"

Chapter 3

Drawings, Sketches, and Paintings

Over the years, Ed produced a myriad of drawings, sketches, and paintings. Many of these reside today at the Ed Pusick Gallery of Montcalm Community College. Included in this collection is his personal drafting table. Gallery curator and adjunct instructor of visual arts, Debbie Bell comments, "Overall this display shows us both the tragic events that happened while out on dangerous water mixed with Ed's witty personality executed so beautifully" (Bell). While most of Ed's later works depicted shipwrecks or maritime scenes, his art included everything from portraits, to architectural drawings, to humorous cartoons. Bell states, "I notice a great sense of comicality within most all Ed's non-maritime titles and definitely in his cartoon illustrations. In *The Executive Suite* the artist depicts himself busily drawing at his drafting table. Ed tastefully slips in puns within posters and signs above and behind his character that are so hilarious!" How ironic that this comical and witty man became known as the Master of Disaster with his absolute mastery of maritime tragedies. These maritime illustrations became the works that ultimately defined Ed's career. The following information (with granted permission) appeared in a promotional brochure created by Frederick Stonehouse that advertised Mr. Pusick's limited edition shipwreck prints of his original drawings and sketches. (Additional commentary has been added.) As a point of information, the term "Remarqued Print" refers to a limited edition personalized...

print issued with an original pencil drawing by the artist in the margin, each numbered out of the quantity of individually remarqued prints in the edition. The quantity of remarqued prints in any one edition generally is between 25 and 50. Each remarque drawing made by the artist is slightly different, thus making each print totally unique. Remarqued prints may be available at the time of publication, or announced at a later date, depending upon the artist's work load at the time. An artist remarqued print is the ultimate collector item in terms of reproduced work. (Somethingforyoursoul.com)

Historic Shipwreck Scenes

Shipwrecks Unlimited is extremely proud to continue to offer its Historic Shipwreck Series of quality black and white prints. Each print is reproduced on high quality paper and is eminently suitable for framing. Each is a remarkable piece of Great Lakes maritime art you will be proud to own and display.

The Illustrator

The illustrator is Mr. Edward Pusick of Wyoming, Michigan. Known as the "Master of Disaster" for his preference of illustrating Great Lakes vessels in the act of sinking, he is one of the Midwest's outstanding maritime artists.

Each print is registered and autographed by the artist. A limited number of special "remarqued" prints, in which the artist has added a small sketch further illustrating the disaster, are also available. Each of the remarqued prints is therefore unique.

Act now to obtain one of these very special prints for your collection. Due to the small number produced, they will not be available for long.

The Series

The Historic Shipwreck Series is a visual history of Great Lakes shipwrecks through the medium of high quality black and white prints. Only a very limited number of prints of each shipwreck is made. The series is an outstanding collection illustrating the Great Lakes' maritime post. Since each print in the series is a limited edition, the value of each will doubtlessly increase with time. A permanent registry of ownership of each print is maintained and as new prints in the series are introduced, previous purchasers will be given the first opportunity to add them to their collections, before the prints are opened for public sale.

The Whitefish Point Collection

The "Whitefish Point Collection" is a very special new collection of prints on the subject of the maritime history of Lake Superior's terrible shipwreck coast. Over fifty vessels met their end in these treacherous waters. Periodically new prints will be introduced into the collection, each illustrating a particular aspect of disaster off Whitefish.

The Edmund Fitzgerald in Storm

The most dramatic shipwreck in modern Great Lakes history occurred on the storm driven night of November 10, 1975 when the 729-foot Edmund Fitzgerald literally disappeared with all hands.

The huge freighter was down-bound from Superior with ore

when she was overtaken by a terrific Lake Superior nor'wester. Battered by 30-foot seas, the Fitzgerald sank without warning 15 miles from Whitefish Point. The tragic sinking of the Fitzgerald has become part of the Great Lakes legend.

The print illustrates the Fitzgerald being overwhelmed by the raging seas, moments before her plunge into history.

Particulars:
Black & White Print. 250 in Edition.
Image size 8" x13½" - Overall size:12 x 16.
Registered & autographed; or registered, autographed, and remarqued.
The legend of the Edmund Fitzgerald remains the most mysterious and controversial of all shipwreck tales heard around the Great Lakes. The Edmund Fitzgerald was lost with her entire crew of 29 men. Her story is surpassed in books, film and media only by that of the Titanic ("The Edmund Fitzgerald").

Art professor and visual arts coordinator Carolyn Johnson reflects, "Not all lake tragedies are fortunate to be remembered in song, and songwriter Gordon Lightfoot has given us a well-told tale that may give us a glimpse into all of the Great Lakes losses. Ed Pusick has certainly given us the visuals of those struggles" (Johnson) She then quotes:

> The legend lives on from the Chippewa on down
> of the big lake they called "Gitche Gumee."
> The lake, it is said, never gives up her dead
> when the skies of November turn gloomy.
> Does anyone know where the love of God goes
> when the waves turn the minutes to hours?
>   -The Wreck of the Edmund Fitzgerald by
>   Gordon Lightfoot (Johnson)

On April 15, 1977 the U.S. Coast Guard released its official report of "Subject: S.S. Edmund Fitzgerald, official number 277437, sinking in Lake Superior on 10 November 1975 with loss of life." While the Coast Guard said the cause of the sinking could not be conclusively determined, it maintained that "the most probable cause of the sinking of the S.S. Edmund Fitzgerald was the loss of buoyancy and stability resulting from massive flooding of the cargo hold. The flooding of the cargo hold took place through ineffective hatch closures as boarding seas rolled along the spar deck."

...Whitefish Point is the site of the Whitefish Point Light Station and Great Lakes Shipwreck Museum. The Great Lakes Shipwreck Historical Society (GLSHS) has conducted three underwater expeditions to the wreck, 1989, 1994, and 1995.

At the request of family members surviving her crew, Fitzgerald's 200 lb. bronze bell was recovered by the Great Lakes Shipwreck Historical Society on July 4, 1995. This expedition was conducted jointly with the National Geographic Society, Canadian Navy, Sony Corporation, and Sault Ste. Marie Tribe of Chippewa Indians. The bell is now on display in the Great Lakes Shipwreck Museum as a memorial to her lost crew. (http://www.shipwreckmuseum.com)

The Blazing Manhattan

The 252-foot wooden steamer Manhattan had sheltered behind Grand Island from a screaming norther' on October 24, 1903. When the winds fell off the following day, the steamer hauled anchor and about midnight started on her way only to have her steering chains break, causing her to run hard up on a rock reef in the East Channel. The force of the collision knocked an oil lantern over, starting a fire that, driven by the still high winds, burned the steamer to her waterline.

The crew escaped without injury with the help of a local fish tug. Subsequent gales destroyed the Manhattan. Today, the remains are eagerly explored by scuba divers.

The print dramatically shows the Manhattan ablaze from stem to stern in her final agony of death. Beneath the illustration is a text fully describing the circumstances of loss.

Particulars
Black & White Print. 250 in Edition.
Image size: 5 5/8" x 8 ½" - Overall size: 12 x 16
Registered & autographed.
Registered, autographed, & remarqued.

The Gilchrist steamer MANHATTAN, downbound on Lake Superior from Duluth for Buffalo, was forced by north gales to shelter behind Grand Island. After the weather moderated late on the night of the 25th, the MANHATTAN started down the east channel for the open lake. About midnight, when she was opposite the Beacon Light, her steering chain broke, causing her to veer off course and strike a reef just off the channel.

No sooner had she struck, a fire broke out. Apparently the

force of the grounding knocked over a lantern which started the conflagration. It was the only explanation the captain and his mates could offer. When the fire could not be brought under control, the crew was taken off by the Powell and Mitchell tug WARD. The steamer burned to the water's edge, and together with her cargo of 76,000 bushels of wheat, was a total loss.

The 1,545-ton MANHATTAN, a comparatively modern and staunch vessel, was built in Detroit in 1887 and measured 252 feet by 38 feet by 19 feet. She had two decks and three masts...

Due to the actions of the salvagers, as well as the destructive forces of the lake's wind and ice, the remains of the MANHATTAN are widely spread along the west side of the east channel. The shallowest sections, in about 15 feet of water, can often be seen from the surface.

Scuba divers can visit a large portion of the steamer's hull framing, including massive timbers and the distinctive iron strapping, in about 25 feet. The vessel's enormous rudder, with its depth markings still visible, lies nearby, along with some of the deck fittings and machinery. Additional portions of the hull can be found farther out in the channel in depths down to 40 feet. (www.shipwrecktours.com)

It Wasn't A Good Day For A Trip On the Lake

"It Wasn't A Good Day For A Trip On the Lake" is the next of our "Whitefish Point Collection," detailing the many disasters of Lake Superior's infamous shipwreck coast. The print portrays the final minutes of the 298-foot steamer Alexander Nimick, wrecked west of Whitefish Point on September 20, 1907.

Particulars:
Black & White Print. 200 in Edition.
Image Size: 9" x14" - Overall Size; 15 x 20.
Registered & autographed.
Registered, autographed, & remarqued.

Debbie Bell comments on *It Wasn't A Good Day for a Trip on the Lake:*

Energy and movement dominates this scene with directional lines- for example; the leaning masts give this painting severe motion. Various degrees of light and dark graphite help give depth and show movement of the turbulent waves of Lake Superior. You can almost feel and hear the waves crashing as they appear to thrust the boats across the drawing. There is a beautiful sensitivity with the materials used. Ed's use of graphite leaves us in awe with his smooth gradation of value that is so polished that it appears photo-realistic. (Bell)

The ALEXANDER NIMICK (official number 106702) was built in 1890 by James Davidson in West Bay City, MI. The wooden vessel measured 298.33 ft. length x 40 ft. width x 21 ft. height, with a gross tonnage of 1968.83, and net tonnage of 1632.03.

The ALEXANDER NIMICK was stranded thirteen miles west of Vermilion Point, MI, Lake Superior, on September 21, 1907; six of seventeen lives were lost. The vessel was bound from Buffalo, NY, for Duluth, MN, with a cargo of coal at the time of loss.

She pressed on for Duluth in a gale after sheltering behind Whitefish Pt. for a day, and then was driven on a bar 13 miles west of Vermilion Pt. The survivors made it to shore in a lifeboat. The vessel was pounded to pieces in 26 feet of water, near the mouth of Two-hearted River, MI. (http://www.whitefishpoint. net/Shipwrecks/shipwrecks.html)

The ship's builder, James Davidson, began shipbuilding operations at West Bay City in 1871 with the building of the schooner E. M. DAVIDSON at the site where the Fletcher Oil is now located. The following year, he relocated his yard in Saginaw. Finding that location unfavorable to shipbuilding, Captain Davidson returned to Bay City in 1873, purchased a site at the foot of Randolph street and began building a sawmill and laying the keel of the steamship JAMES DAVIDSON...

In January 1888, Davidson completed a new band mill which was "the most thoroughly modern ship mill in the United States" and supplied it with the latest improved machinery for working heavy timber and improved punches for heavy iron work. Fire completely destroyed the new band mill in August of the same year. The premises were immediately rebuilt, however, and furnished with additional tools and appliances to meet the needs of the yard. (http://www.wrecksite.eu)

They Lost the Struggle

One of the unsolved mysteries of the Great Lakes involves the strange double loss of the steamers Regina and Charles S. Price. Both were lost with all hands on Lake Huron on November 9, 1913, during a tremendous storm.

What was so puzzling was the strange fact that when the bodies of crewmen from the Price washed ashore, they were clad in lifejackets clearly marked Regina! At last report, both vessels were widely separated.

The print depicts a possible solution to the mystery; the vessels collided during the height of the storm, enabling crewmen on the Price to either reach the Regina decks or man one of her transferred lifeboats...which was later capsized!

Particulars:
Black & White Print. 250 in Edition.
Image size: 10" x 16 5/8" – Overall size: 16 x 21 ½.
Registered & autographed.
Registered, autographed, & remarqued.
Commenting on *They Lost the Struggle*, Debbie Bell shares, "I notice a man overboard reaching out, and those within the lifeboat struggling to save him pull at our emotions as well. Trying to control the uncontrollable is a theme in life, and Pusick captures this powerfully" (Bell).

When Things Get Out of Hand

"When Things Get Out of Hand" is the first print in the new "Whitefish Point Collection." It represents the many small schooners lost along the lonely Whitefish Coast. The print graphically depicts a two-masted schooner trapped and dying on an offshore reef. It is considered by the artist to be his finest effort. The subtlety of tone and overall expression will not be fully appreciated by all.

The print is intended for those true maritime art lovers with the ability to comprehend the quality of this unique work.

Particulars:
Black & White print. 200 in Edition.
Image Size; 9" x 14" Overall Size:15 x 20.
Registered & autographed.
Registered, autographed, & remarqued.

Of all of the works now on exhibit at the Montcalm Community College Ed Pusick Gallery, this is the painting that most fascinates Carolyn Johnson:

As I first looked at Ed Pusick's shipwreck artwork, I was struck by how appropriately it fell into a long history of "dangerous seas" artistic expressions. Looking at Pusick's *When Things Got Out of Hand*, my first visual connection was to the famous painting by Rembrandt, *Christ in the Storm on the Sea of Galilee*. A similar feeling of being tempest-tossed was communicated to me with an urgency and an immediacy that made the event seem very real, and that Pusick must have been an eye witness to be able to capture it so vividly. Unfortunately, there is no calm, glowing and serene figure like Christ in Pusick's print. It must have been a very bleak experience on that ship.

By the shading in the murky sky, we see a subtle change of value on the left as the storm rises from that direction. The masts at a 45 degree angle also remind me of the turmoil in the Rembrandt painting, as the ships in both images are tossed to the right. Amid all the clouds and sea spray, the detail of line shows distinctly the taut ropes of the masts and cross pieces, straining to stay tied together.

Pusick's command of depicting water is masterful. His use of value, shading and shape bring out the three dimensional feeling and pulls the viewer into the picture by making it appear as though we are at the same level and in the same roiling water as the foundering ship. There is a tiny lifeboat with a mere 4 people on it, struggling to make it to shrouded safety on the spit of wooded land that juts into the picture plane from the right side. We also see an ominous floating board in the foregrounded water, at the same angle as the ship, giving a glimpse of the inevitable breaking up of the once majestic vessel.

The attention to detail, the centering of the ship with its diagonal pitch, the crashing waves, and the implied haven on the right give us a glimpse of an exciting story of man and nature. (Johnson)

Disaster at the Pictured Rocks

The sidewheeler Superior was upbound on Superior on October 30, 1856, when she fell victim to a roaring north gale. Lashed by the violent seas, the Superior was disabled and helplessly driven against the towering cliffs of the Pictured Rocks near Spray Falls. Forty of her passengers and crew met death in the disaster. A mere 16 survivors were able to climb the rocks to temporary safety. After a 25-mile trek through deep snow they reached help at settlers' cabins on Grand Island.

The print shows the once proud Superior as she is being destroyed against the Pictured Rocks.

Particulars
Black & White Print. 250 in Edition.
lmagesize:10" x 16" - Overall size 16 x 20.
Registered & autographed.
Registered, autographed, and marqued.

The following articles announced this disaster:

Steamer SUPERIOR, cargo supplies and passengers, lost rudder and drifted ashore on Lake Superior, in a severe gale. Total loss. 35 lives lost.

Buffalo Commercial Advertiser, January 31, 1857 (1856 casualty list)…

STEAMER LOST. - By a gentleman from Lake Superior, says the Detroit Tribune we learn that the steamer SUPERIOR, Capt. Jones, from Chicago for Superior City and intermediate ports, is supposed to be lost. She passed through the canal, bound up, Oct 29th, and it is supposed she went down the next day or night, somewhere near Grand Island, with all on board. Vessels have been partially around the lake since, and nothing has been heard of her. She had about 30 passengers. There was a severe gale on the 30th, which strengthens the surmise. The SUPERIOR was an old boat, and would not be able to stand a very heavy storm.

Buffalo Daily Republic, Wednesday, November 12, 1856...

LOSS OF THE STEAMER SUPERIOR - THIRTY FIVE LIVES LOST.

We learn from a private dispatch dated Detroit, Nov, 14, that the loss of the steamer SUPERIOR, in Lake Superior, is but too true. The dispatch says that she was wrecked off Pictorial Rocks and thirty-five lives were lost. Only nineteen were saved, among whom the only officers were the mate and engineer. We shall probably have further intelligence by telegraph before going to press.

Buffalo Daily Republic, Saturday, November 15, 1856 (http://images.maritimehistoryofthegreatlakes.ca)

Ed often added his own commentary to this disaster, explaining one account he heard that some surviving crew members had abandoned their passengers. Some of these passengers swam to an island but froze to death soon afterward. Evidently, those crew members responsible were later spotted in a Munising bar but never prosecuted.

Steamer on the Reef: The Herman H. Hettler

While attempting to reach shelter in Munising Bay, Lake Superior, from a vicious north gale, the 211-foot wooden steamer Herman H. Hettler ran hard upon a rock reef. The disaster occurred on the night of November 23, 1926.

Although all of her 16-man crew were saved, the ship was doomed. Later winter storms shattered her until nothing was left above the water. Today, the wreck is a popular target of scuba divers.

The print dramatically illustrates the Hettler high on the reef as the storm waves sweep over her decks. In the background the last of her crew is leaving by lifeboat. Beneath the illustration is a text fully describing the circumstances of loss.

Particulars
Black & White Print. 250 in edition.
Image size: 6 ¾" x 10 3/8" - Overall size: 12 x 16.
Registered & autographed.
Registered, autographed, & remarqued.

Debbie Bell reflects on this piece:

"Steamer on the Reef" is another of my favorites. This drawing shows the enormous scale of the steamer structure that escapes the grips of treacherous waters because of the small life boat with clutching figures within it. Pencil is a simple art tool that is many times used merely for plotting things out for other materials to then take over. But Ed found graphite not just useful as a guide but took it on as his choice of media and took control of it. (Bell)

More on the story behind this sketch is posted online:

On November 23, 1926, the 36 year old wooden steamer HERMAN H. HETTLER was seeking shelter in Munising Harbor from a fall gale when a reported compass variation caused her to veer off course and slam into the rock reef off Trout Point, at the north end of the east channel. The HETTLER, under Captain John M. Johnson, was en route from Ludington, Michigan to Duluth with a cargo of 1,100 tons of bulk table salt. The accident happened about 8:30 p.m. while visibility was restricted by heavy snow squalls.

The force of the grounding was so severe that it ran the steamer on the rocks up to her third hatch and forced her bow three feet out of the water! The seas were slamming into the HETTLER regularly, causing the steamer to "work" on the rocks, and slowly but steadily opening her seams. Blowing his whistle to attract attention, the captain kept his 16 man crew aboard and worked the pumps. The following day, when it was obvious the steamer wasn't going anywhere, they launched their lifeboats, which were towed into Munising by the fishing tug PREBLE.

From town the captain notified the vessel's owners and wired for assistance from the Great Lakes Towing Company.

After returning to the HETTLER on the 25th, the captain reported her nearly a total loss. She had pounded badly and opened many of her seams. The cargo hold was awash and the salt was rapidly dissolving! The next storm was expected to break the wreck completely. Wrecking tugs were sent for, but they were needed elsewhere to assist newer, more valuable vessels, so the aged steamer was left to fend for herself. This spelled the end for the HERMAN H. HETTLER. (http:// shipwrecktours.com/shipwrecks/the-herman-hettler/)

John M. Osborn

On the warm evening of July 27, 1884 the steam barge John M. Osborn was in heavy fog, nearing Whitefish Point with a load of iron ore from Marquette, Michigan. She was towing two schooner-barges, the George W. Davis and the Thomas Gawn.

Captain Thomas Wilford dutifully sounded the Osborn's whistle at the required three blasts every two minutes. Fog does strange things at sea - for all of a sudden, Captain Wilford heard an answering blast from another vessel, very close at hand.

In the next moment, the steel prow of the fast Canadian Pacific steamer Alberta came out of the fog like a spectre, headed straight for the Osborn's starboard side! Both vessels had been traveling faster than practical in poor visibility; both had checked their speed down upon hearing each other's whistles, but it was too late. The Alberta crashed into the Osborn aft on the starboard side near the boiler room.

People aboard each ship realized the force of the collision had locked the vessels together. Passengers and crew from the doomed Osborn raced to clamber aboard the bow of the Alberta. One of the Alberta's passengers, a seaman headed to join his own ship at Port Arthur, Ontario, felt confident enough to jump from the safety of the Alberta to rescue an injured Osborn crewman scalded in the engine room as a result of the collision.

His heroic action cost him his life. For just as the rescuer made it into the Osborn's engine room, the ships separated, and the Osborn instantly dove to the bottom, taking him and three of the Osborn's crew with her. Survivors were taken by the Alberta to the Soo, and the Osborn's tows were picked up by another passing steam barge. The story closed with a decision by U.S. District Court in Detroit determining that "both vessels were at fault and that damages shall be divided equally between them."

(http://www.shipwreckmuseum.com/johnmosborn)

Come travel 170 feet below icy Lake Superior to investigate a 100-year-old shipwreck.

Markers and Publications

Ed's powerful sketches and drawings made their way into museums, lighthouses, university campuses, government offices, art councils, private homes, The History Channel, academic journals, book covers, and historical markers. Here are a few examples from the shores of Lake Huron, Lake Superior, the *Shipwreck Journal*, and a history book on *Shipwrecks of the Straits of Mackinac* by Dr. Charles and Jeri Feltner.

Memorial marker on the Straights of Mackinac (Lake Huron) at St. Ignace, MI
Illustrated by Ed Pusick

Graveyard of the Great Lakes

Ed Pusick

Whitefish Point has been called the graveyard of Lake Superior. Since navigation began on Lake Superior there has been approximately 550 wrecks. More vessels were lost in the Whitefish Point area than any other part of Lake Superior. There are three major reasons for the high loss of ships in the Whitefish Point area. First, the eastern end of the lake is very congested where the lake narrows down like a funnel and up and down bound ship traffic must pass. Poor visibility in this congested area from fog, forest fires, and snow has caused numerous collisions and groundings. Finally, the nature of the largest lake itself, with the great expanse of over 200 miles of open water can build up terrific seas during a Superior "Northwestern" storm.

Collisions were more common in earlier times because there were more vessels. In the 1880's over 3100 commercial vessels were on the lakes compared to less than 200 today. Since the first known shipwreck of a commercial vessel, the Invincible, in November 1816 to the Edmund Fitzgerald on November 10, 1975, approximately 320 lives have been lost in over 300 shipwrecks and accidents in the area known as the graveyard of the Great Lakes.

Outdoor Placard at Whitefish Point, MI, illustrated by Ed Pusick

Lois T. Hauck & Gary L. Hauck

SHIPWRECK JOURNAL

The Quarterly Journal of the
Great Lakes Shipwreck Historical Society

Volume 9 / Number 3   **Summer 1992**

Lost to the Gale

Journal cover illustration by Ed Pusick
(Used with permission)

SHIPWRECKS

OF THE

STRAITS

OF

MACKINAC

Dr. Charles E. Feltner & Jeri Baron Feltner

Book cover illustration by Ed Pusick
(Used with permission)

Other Maritime Drawings

In addition to his limited edition shipwreck drawings, Pusick did a number of less-detailed works of ships that had not wrecked, or at least, not yet. These works are now on display in the Ed Pusick Gallery of Montcalm Community College, Sidney, Michigan.

Ships

John Mitchell

THE SEVERED SCHOONER

IT WASN'T A GOOD TIME FOR SHIPS TO PASS IN THE NIGHT, NOT AT LEAST FOR TWO VES
SELS IN THE PREDAWN OF AUGUST 9, 1862. ON THAT DATE A LARGE STEAMER, TH
ILLINOIS, COLLIDED WITH A SCHOONER IN THE FOG OFF GRAND ISLAND LIGHT. THE
ISLAND IS IN LAKE SUPERIOR DIRECTLY TO THE NORTH OF MUNISING.

THE SIDEWHEELER ILLINOIS, A CRACK PASSENGER STEAMER OF HER TIME, HAD BEEN
ENCOUNTERING INTERMITTENT FOG ON THE UP BOUND VOYAGE, ACCORDING TO HER OF
CERS, AND THEY GAVE THIS REASON FOR NOT SOUNDING THE VESSEL'S FOG WHISTLE.

ALTHOUGH THE STEAMER SUSTAINED EXTENSIVE BOW DAMAGE FROM THE COLLISIO
SHE WAS FOUND TO BE STILL SEAWORTHY, BUT NO EFFORT WAS MADE TO ASCERTAIN
THE EXTENT OF DAMAGES TO THE UNKNOWN SCHOONER. THE STEAMER'S MASTER
WAS MORE CONCERNED WITH THE SAFETY OF HIS 150 PASSENGERS AMONGST WHOM
WAS THE MAYOR OF DETROIT, AND THE ILLINOIS STEAMED AWAY TO MARQUETTE

Missoula

Huronton

Edmund Fitzgerald

John M. Osborn
with barge tow

M.M. Drake

Miztec

Myron

William F. Sauber

Alexander Nimick

Aurania

Early clipper schooner type
circa 1855
They averaged 90 to 100 feet in length.
The clipper schooners were noted for their
seaworthiness and fast speed – up to 20 miles
per hour.

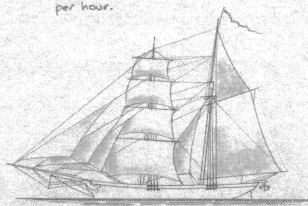

A Great Lakes brigantine
circa 1855
Employed as bulk freight carriers of
iron ore and grain. Sailors called
them "brigs". They averaged about
95 feet in length. The first ocean
saltie (oceangoing vessel) to sail on
the Great Lakes was the Britisher
Madeira Pet, a brigantine similar
to the above.

Other Sketches, Drawings, and Paintings (Non-maritime)

In addition to his shipwreck and maritime drawings, Pusick did a number of humorous sketches (including several of himself), several mysterious illustrations, and a handful of comical "doodles." Two of his favorite non-maritime drawings were of his "Caribbean Office," and "The Investigator." In his "Caribbean Office," one can notice his crutches leaning against the bar.

This was my busy office complex in Jamaica, W.I., during Sept. of 85. It featured a lot of wacky birds including a colony of stray, nondescript beach cats. The hotdogs and hamburgers were bad although the drinking water was excellent. 10-23-05 Ed

Ed's "Caribbean Office"

According to Fred Stonehouse, "The Investigator" is also an illustration of a true story. He explains, "Years following the wreck of the ship *Alpena,* an officer's cap from the company was found in the dunes...still in the grasp of a skeletal hand" (Stonehouse, 27 Jan. 2013).

He also produced numerous paintings and pastels of homes, furniture, fashions, stained-glass windows, decal-designs, and flowers. Bell comments on one of his architectural drawings, "This is an excellent example of 2 pt. perspective. Symmetry prevails in this structure as it makes one feel safe and secure, and therefore welcomed" (Bell).

A Drawing from Ed's Portfolio

Ships and Sailors

From the time I was a small boy, until long after I had grown to manhood, I don't recall that I ever heard anyone say much about the Great Lakes. My earliest recollection, during the 1930's, was that in several of the small towns near Lake Michigan one could find good smoked fish for sale. Except for a ferry ride across the Straits of Mackinac, and enjoying an occasional swim at Muskegon Beach, that was about all I knew of the lakes. I glimpsed a few steamers, and as a youngster, growing up in Battle Creek, I would sometimes hear people make disparaging remarks about sailors, indicating they were individuals to be shunned. Nobody ever mentioned the word ships and any vessel, large or small, was called a "boat". Maritime disasters were things that were said to occur on distant oceans and anything going on in the lakes, or their maritime communities, was about as remote from me as the moon.

The timeless fresh-water seas, awesomely vast and lonely, have seen over 300 years of navigational history, but as long as there are ships and sailors to man them, they will challenge their supremacy.

C. Pusick

Maritime Illustrator
Great Lakes shipwrecks

Dec. 12
19 81

Chapter 4

Writings

In addition to being a talented artist, Ed Pusick was also a gifted writer. Though none of his writings have been published until now, one can readily see his craft as a wordsmith in the journals, poems, essays, and letters that he left behind. Many of these selections are also autobiographical in nature, or demonstrate his love for his work, history, country, and/or maritime folklore. The following are samples of these pieces:

The Glorious Dream

And from out of the darkness came a light,
Closer still it wandered.
From out its source, oh so right,
Brilliant rays ascended.
That I with doubtless fears pretending,
Shall never know what did becalm me.
For seemingly endless realm of voices,
Consoled my doubts,
And forced my eyes to seek the mystic powers of this divinity.

Then ere from distant beam of light,
A thrilling sound enchanced me.
No brighter light have yet I've seen,
But as the likeness of the sun.
Transformed in a moving mass of fire,
While without an azure circle hove,
With bits of orange between,
Added a final touch of scenic beauty,
A lasting thought to guide me.

And then with music, vibrant yet sweet,
I with joyous heart arose,
To advance in a new found world yet so old,
But when then I started, I was becalmed,
And thought I tried and tried again,
I knew at last with vagrant heart,
That this was but a grand Amen.

And from out this vision I felt a calm
Within my soul – a peace and quiet,
My fears of hated death abashed.
And like the light that now grew dim,
I knew at last what lay before me.
Edward Pusick

First Designs

The first color rendering which relates to Great Lakes Maritime History was titled "Ghosts of the Voyageurs." I completed the work in the early months of 1978 and it was given to Mr. Thomas J. Barnes.

Later that spring, at the request of Mr. Michael O. McFarlin, I executed the picture which I called, "Last Voyage of the Edmund Fitzgerald." This was my first attempt to depict a vessel which met with disaster in the Great Lakes [as mentioned in more detail in Chapter

2]. The successful completion of this rendering inspired me to do "The Ghost of the Christmas Tree Ship." This picture was given to Mr. Robert E. Brady.

As work progressed on the X-Mas Tree Ship, I contemplated doing a shipwreck scene for the U.S. Coast Guard. They had afforded me their generous assistance, furnishing me with technical information regarding wave action, icing, distress signals, and ships running lights.

I commenced a color sketch of the sinking of the steamer Chicora, which sank in Lake Michigan in 1895. The picture was not completed when I gave it to Chief T. J. Thompson, U.S.C.G., Grand Haven, Michigan Station. Chief Thompson was the "Officer In Charge" of the station. It was then about May of 1978 and shortly thereafter I did the rendering of the U.S.C.G. motor lifeboat on a rescue mission. I called this picture, "They Who Go Out," and I presented it to the Grand Haven Station in July.

The decision was then made to render a series of pastel renderings depicting ill-fated ships of the Great Lakes, which would be donated to public institutions and governmental agencies. A record of some of the presentations is as follows:

1. The Bannockburn Phantom (Donated to Kentwood Library, 1978)
2. The Burning Seabird (Donated to Wyoming Library, 1978)
3. The Wreck on South Fox Island (Donated to Dept. of Natural Resources, 1978)
4. The Foundering Lumberhooker (Was to be donated to the Grand Rapids Public Museum)
5. The Doomed Whaleback James P. Colgate (Donated to the Fred Stonehouse Collection)

Ships and Sailors
E. Pusick, Maritime illustrator
Great Lakes shipwrecks
Dec. 12, 1981

From the time I was a small boy, until long after I had grown to manhood, I don't recall that I ever heard anyone say much about the Great Lakes. My earliest recollection, during the 1930's, was that in several of the small towns near Lake Michigan one could find good smoked fish for sale. Except for a ferry ride across the Straits of Mackinac, and enjoying an occasional swim at Muskegon Beach, that was about all I knew of the lakes. I glimpsed a few steamers, and as a youngster, growing up in Battle Creek, I would sometimes hear people make disparaging remarks about sailors, indicating they were individuals to be shunned. Nobody ever mentioned the word ships, and any vessel, large or small, was called a "boat." Maritime disasters were things that were said to occur on distant oceans and anything going on in the lakes, or their maritime communities, was about as remote from me as the moon.

The timeless fresh-water seas, awesomely vast and lonely, have seen over 300 years of navigational history, but as long as there are ships and sailors to man them, they will challenge their supremacy.

A Link to the Past
Ed Pusick
June 28, 1998

After serving in the U. S. Navy during the latter part of World War II, as a reservist, I was recalled to active duty upon the outbreak of the Korean War. Shortly thereafter, I encountered Captain Ernest McSorley at a Jacksonville (Fla.) shipyard and spent a pleasant afternoon with him aboard his vessel, a Liberty-Class ship, one of several from a fleet of moth-balled merchantmen being restored to service there.

During my visit with McSorley, he mentioned that before long he would be the skipper of an ore boat up north, an assignment that would make him the youngest Master (meaning commander) of a merchant vessel on the Great Lakes. Then, in response to my aspiration to become a merchant sailor, he urged me not to pursue a maritime service career. This was a disappointment, because in 1951, at age 24, I considered myself to be an experienced seaman – and boiler-firing coal passer.

Nevertheless, I took McSorley's advice; choosing, instead, to take on many other aspirations, none of which came to fruition. But in the context of that, this is not the fault of the last Master of the Edmund Fitzgerald. [See more on this story in Chapter 2.]

Reflections on a Lake
October 17, 2000

It may be that Battle Creek's Goguac Lake is the most unusual inland lake in our state, perhaps the nation; more so, because of the two revelations you are about to read, and these are not the fanciful musings of a slightly indigent, old storyteller. They are true. One features a giant fish, the other ... a shipwreck!

During the early '30s, my grandfather was among the fortunate few to have glimpsed a legendary, monstrous fish known to exist in Goguac Lake. However, I suppose there are those who will say they know of big fish in other lakes, too, except the one in reference does not compare with their fish stories. Mine is unequaled in magnitude, a boastful disclosure made possible by the fact it was my turn to see the great fish while fishing, along, one summer's day in 1959 on a part of the lake said to be its habitat. The seemingly ageless fish – or was it a later version? – was observed at length under bright sunlight in clear water, a fathom deep; and being nothing short of seven feet from head to tail, the subject was large enough to have capsized the eight- foot boat I was in.

Too broad to be classified a sturgeon, my grandfather chose to liken its color and characteristics to that of a dogfish (a small shark). But whatever description fits the best, it would be comforting to learn if that strange, aquatic creature still bottom feeds along the southern boundaries of the lake.

A century ago, a sizeable steam launch often cruised the length of Goguac Lake, although it is uncertain if it was used for hire or the owner's personal pleasure. Nevertheless, following a daylight scenic tour on the lake, the skipper tied his launch to a dock in a location called Peach Cove at the time. But, later, during the night, a fire broke out, trapping and killing a young woman passenger who happened to be sleeping aboard. A frantic witness shoved the flaming vessel, now fully engulfed, clear of the dock, the movement assisted by a light northerly breeze; and after drifting for a distance of, roughly, ten yards offshore, the boat's hull timbers parted—and down she went.

That is pretty much the story a beloved aunt of mine used to tell. Old newspaper accounts of the incident may vary, yet one thing is evident: the vessel's burned artifacts are in the lake.

There are events in one's life more memorable than others, and the following account stems from a recollection that has served me well. In fact, it cites an unforgettable experience of my early youth. On the other hand, it is common knowledge some old-timers can recall many things they did when they were young, but never remember what they did yesterday. The reader, of course, should feel free to identify the author as a member of that venerable citizenry.

When I was 13, that same aunt took me for a day of summer fishing on Goguac Lake, and using a rowboat, we made our way to (Peach Cove) where an effort was made to find the sunken remains of the launch. Applying a method learned from her father, my aunt proceeded to position our boat according to a pre-determined set of sight bearings taken on permanent landmarks, a technique which ultimately brought them not only to the wreck site but to one of their favorite fishing grounds, nearby.

As she maneuvered the boat for proper alignment with those locating coordinates, my youthful curiosity kept me alert and watchful. In those days, the water clarity for that small, peaceful corner of the lake was above average, and under sunlit, cloudless skies bottom surfaces were usually discernible, a fathom deep, and that day was no exception; undisturbed, as it were, by the era's watercraft: low and sleek wooden-hulled speedboats which occasionally troubled the water—and fishermen—elsewhere.

Several yards south of the wreck it was said there existed a drop-off wherein schools of mature yellow perch were often found in abundance, given the right time and weather conditions. However, the key to finding this fishing hole lay in determining the wreck's position first, per the locating fix, and not that it was necessary to view its remains. I was simply anxious to cast eye on them.

Although the launch sank to a bottom depth of only four feet or less, I was told the wreckage was no longer easy to spot. Having settled in much, then layered with sediment over the years, a similar shading of the bottom surface and its objects made identification difficult, especially with the addition of aquatic weeds and whenever sunlight was limited. But as it turned out, we soon found the vessels water grave, and the gleamy pigments displayed in the underwater tableaux which greeted us, comprised a sight worthy of remembrance.

Adjacent to a relatively small field of wreckage artifacts were colonies of yellow, gushy submerged weeds, their growth festooned with tiny pearl-white seeds; and though alien to me, these strange plants – rose tinted at their base – wore colors in a semblance of (peach) fruit.

Yet beyond this area and spanning a larger one, examination yielded further surprises. Visible areas of the cove's floor were seemingly carpeted with a yellow-ocher algas (Algas means the same as algae and it is not plural. The description 'yellow-ocher algas' is found in most standard collegiate dictionaries.) tinged with glittering gold and copper hues, accentuated by another indigenous week. The oddity of the latter was that its development was strewn across bottom levels in the form of expansive, stringy stems, each bearing broad but tapering blue-green leafage; and beneath this eye-catching array were glimpses of the old steamer's boiler.

Poking its round, corroded head slightly above the algas, the boiler had a diameter of your average or medium size garbage can lid, and at its center was a gaping hole, the smoke vent which presumable was fitted with a tall funnel, now missing. But next in the order of perceptible objects revealed itself, nearby. This was the partly exposed circular side of what apparently had been the boiler's water supply tank.

Elsewhere, a slight mound of curvature, about 20 feet long, marked the starboard side of the sunken hulk, a conclusion reached by a pair of exposed charred wood pieces shaping a pointed prow or bow end, while the line of that curve obviously represented what was left of a gunwale or gunnel, the latter not to be confused with a slimy fish by that name. The word gunnel is also a nautical term describing a raised frame rail or coaming designed to keep water out, and it was this lineament which, in the case here, offered items of particular significance. Protruding in alignment with the curvature of a hidden gunnel, and spaced at regular intervals, were a number of slender, bent and twisted metal rods suggesting they once supported a wood canopy, principal covering for a steam launch of (that) era.

My curiosity satisfied, we moved to the edge of the drop-off and anchored there. But still pondering what I had witnessed, I asked my aunt – busy at the time impaling small, unruly red worms on dual fishhooks attached separately to catgut leaders –if the woman's body was recovered following the accident. Pausing to lay aside a tall bamboo pole, popular fishing gear in that day, she rested her gaze on the near distant watery location of a long-ago tragic mishap. Then turning to me, she made a statement indicating uncertainty, and sensing her response ended my youthful quest for confirming that unpleasant part of the occurrence, I proceeded to bait a hook with some of those same red worms selected from a can of orchard manure. Tiny by comparison to the other angle-worm species, it was my grandfather who observed that when the former bait was pierced they produced a mustard-like secretion, the taste of which drove pan fish into a feeding frenzy. Problem was (and members of P.E.T.A. might appreciate this) clever fish could, without provocation, easily strip such food morsels from the hooks of unwary or unskilled fishermen. Moreover, the task of threading those exceptionally thin, wriggly invertebrates on short-shank fishhooks proved tougher than expected, the sharp barbs missing their purpose more often than not. In point of fact, the lunch I served to the perch was less punctured than my fingers were, presenting altogether a distressful dilemma leading to frustration, and lacking any prior, successful hands on experience, my hope for having a nice day was fading.

Meanwhile, the worms' yellow residue and fertilizer clung tenaciously to one's hand digits, the mixture eventually smearing a bologna sandwich previously withheld for emergency food replenishment; suitable bread topping more or less for a sun baked, novice fisherman learning how to tough things out, contamination or appearance of it notwithstanding. But at this juncture, as if needed, my aunt took the opportunity to divert and relieve a harried teen from a hopelessly wormy preoccupancy. Unfortunately, that relief was short-lived.

Apparently challenged by the earlier question and dwelling on it, she renewed a topic relating to my former keen interest, namely; the launch incident, embracing withal a weighed disclosure hitherto unthought-of in my philosophy. In other words, I was about to be enlightened, if nothing else. After adjusting a ribbon hatband on her wide brim straw hat, a shade sheltering device no self-respecting kid would wear, my seasoned fishing partner opened the discussion. Our brief conversation went like this:

"The woman who died on the boat was a hospital nurse," she said. "Oh," I replied, and confident of making a point, I asked rather skeptically: "Well, if the lady was smart enough to be a nurse, why didn't she jump over the side when the thing caught fire?" "No," my aunt countered, she was caught asleep in a deck cabin or enclosure of some kind." Momentarily silent then, my aunt sipped water from a mason jar, one of two we brought containing that vital provision, except no thought had been given for keeping it cool. But seemingly refreshed, she summarized her narrative with this startling assessment: "Burnt for a longtime in a fire like that, there wouldn't have been much left of her to recover." The mental imagery conjured up by those words framed my decision not to go there with any further questions.

We had been on the lake about six hours, fishing a short distance removed from (the) cove. As a hot afternoon wore on, my aunt was reaching her catch limit while my fish stringer held a meager collection of five or so blue gills, which may indicate perch are smarter than the blue gill species. After all, I was just a learner in the sport, a bungling one at best. Then, to my relief, a cool, brisk wind commenced to ripple surface water around our boat, and glances at a darkening western sky told us a storm was due, the feathery tentacles of an ominous-looking (anvil-head) cloud already overhead. It was time for a couple of weary anglers to leave the lake.

Epilogue

During that summer of 1940—aside from being skunked by a bunch of fish—a number of things troubled me. I hated my part-time caretaker's job at a lady's estate, along with festering dog bite wounds inflicted on my left leg; and worse yet, public education mandated that my next semester class attendance would start at a big high school where bigger kids might pose a threat.

A second great war was shaping up in Europe making "Blitzkrieg" an important vocabulary entry for a word to be dreaded. Meanwhile, in the U.S., most of President Roosevelt's 'New Deal' programs were languishing, but who would have believed at the time it would take a war to restore this nation's economy; and before dying the year before, my father foretold of a day, soon, when America's military met those of Imperial Japan in combat covering a wide expanse of the Pacific Ocean and its rim. Remembering his prediction, I secretly harbored a selfish desire, that should those hostilities occur, they would continue long enough for me to enlist in our navy. Mine was a wish fulfilled.

Biographical Notes

The aunt in my narratives was Olive, daughter of Ed Sampson, my grandfather. His other daughter Bessie, was my mother.

Henry Sampson, the sister's grandfather was among the first to settle in a wilderness place called Harmonia, site of present-day Fort Custer Industrial Park, located just west of Battle Creek. This patriarchal pioneer descended from a boy orphan named Sampson, one of a hundred-odd passengers aboard the Mayflower, a small but reliable sailing vessel which crossed the Atlantic in 1620, landing at Plymouth Rock, a large and somewhat flat boulder standing in what is now the resort City of Plymouth; Massachusetts.

Although only half of the original pilgrims were still alive the following year, those surviving... male members... at least, became known as the Pilgrim Father. This may account for the reason I feel ancient at times, Thanksgiving Day in particular.

Some Things Tend to Resurface
Edward Pusick
May 14, 2004

The (miniature) 1977 special limited edition commemorative print series featuring the ore carrier, Edmund Fitzgerald, in heavy seas was one of five illustrations which I rendered, initially, for a 1990 PBS film documentary sponsored by the Great Lakes Historical Society.

Unfortunately, the video was never completed. Both the producer and director of the show believed my work was unfaithful to the final hours of the "Fitz;" that my scenes depicted the huge vessel in an unrealistic manner.

But seven years later, while downsizing a vast file collection of preliminary sketch ideas, unpublished manuscripts, vessel photocopy and memorabilia, etc., I uncovered a screen for making a printing mat (or plate) of singular importance. The scene imprinted on it was that of the subject. I then recalled that my fondness for the work caused me to order a reduced-size copy, intending at the time to have prints made from it, or at least, copy machine replicas. Even so, the project was deferred and, eventually, forgotten.

However, my discovery of the artifact brought a renewed inspiration not to be denied, and a nearby printing firm soon had the mat and my design information to issue 100 copies of the subject, which I entitled, "Don't Allow Nobody on Deck!"

In 1999, the above was one of two illustrations of mine showcased on the History Channel, and I understand they have since been featured on that TV channel.

Rouse Simmons – A Yuletide Legacy
Edward Pusick

For many years, the three-masted schooner Rouse Simmons was known in Chicago as the "Christmas Tree Ship." That was because her owner and skipper, Herman Schunneman, found it profitable to end his shipping season each year by transporting evergreens to that city from Michigan's Upper Peninsula. But on November 25, 1913, as the aging schooner (her deck piled high with spruce and balsam for the happy holidays) hurried down bound to the "windy city" from Manistique, Michigan, she was overtaken by a fierce storm causing winds of gale force nine to rip across Lake Michigan.

The following day, an ice-covered Rouse Simmons, displaying tattered sails and distress signals, was sighted in monstrous waves off Sturgeon Bay, Wisconsin, and though a valiant effort was made to rescue her crew, the stricken vessel soon vanished in a snow squall, never to be seen again, on the Great Lakes.

For fifteen (15) prior years, a nameless skid row derelict had assisted Captain Schunneman of the vessel by selling his Christmas trees in downtown Chicago. He was observed by witnesses to have waited for days for the ship to come it. He disbelieved reports of its sinking. On Christmas morning he was found frozen to death at the end of the Clark Street dock.

The next spring, however, hundreds of evergreens began to litter the Wisconsin beaches; and many of them having fouled the nets of commercial fishermen, prompted the latter to issue angry complaints at the offices of both state and federal authorities. Meanwhile, the trees – shorn of their foliage – continued to drift ashore…all summer long!

A Fond Remembrance
(Do milkweeds produce milk? ~ A question
I asked when I was a child ~)
By
Edward Pusick
November 10, 2004

Many are those who love a mystery, especially one that defies a solution. The following mystery carries that tradition, and the subject of it served as the introduction to a hastily prepared speech I gave on a warm, sunny afternoon to a meeting of six commissioners of the Michigan Department of Natural Resources and 400 or so, invited public guests, including some members of the press and those representing outdoor magazine media. The date was September 7, 1978, and the location was at the DNR Higgins Lake auditorium, situated in a scenic, wooded area on the north side of the lake.

About two weeks prior to my presentation, which included a large pastel rendering of mine to the DNR, entitled, "The Wreck on South Fox Island," it was my decision to search for the true story of the two-masted lake schooner depicted in the illustration; the most splendid scene I ever created in the pastel medium: a chalk-like substance; except, I worked it using a rare friction/bonding technique, making the picture resemble an oil painting.

Initially, I had by chance, uncovered an eye-catching three-by-four inch, black and white, photocopy of the subject vessel in an outdated paperback marine history book (of no-name recollection). Pictured without identification, the sole caption read that it was "a schooner wreck on South Fox Island." The noticeable damage was that the vessel's wooden hull was stove in at the bow, just below the waterline: perhaps, reason for beaching the "doomed" fore-and-aft (sail) rigged ship. Furnished with this evidence – together with the remaining, visible, nomenclature – I created a greatly enlarged version of the photocopy, in color, on heavy-ply illustration paper: the scenery reflecting a darkening sky to the west, encroaching a sunlit, abandoned, shipwreck...gentle wave lap...beach sand and grass.

The story of the unknown shipwreck would, I thought, make my speech all the more interesting; thus, some investigative research was needed. So, following a lead, I phoned the Traverse City Public Library and there my quest was put to a librarian who responded by saying my interest in that particular mystery schooner was most odd, because only a week prior an old newspaper clipping describing the wreck of the subject was "stolen" from one of the library's rare document files. She added that she never read the article, but seemed to recall that it was dated about 1913 and the story, "a lengthy one," she continued to say, featured a photocopy of the vessel I described.

Nonetheless, the librarians statements helped to embellish my narrative, prompting me to add (to the DNR assemblage), that it seemed providential that a mysterious, nameless, beached schooner of a bygone era would remain, captured, forever -- a ghostly image in a serene setting.

As I was to learn, milkweed (an erect perennial herb with milky, latex, juice) grows mainly, on an east/west line dividing a northern part of our state, the demarcation centered, more or less, on the small village of Marion, located about 15 miles southeast of the City of Cadillac.

My father explained some of this phenomena to me and my disinterested mother as we journeyed northward on a pleasant midsummer's day from our hometown of Battle Creek, Michigan, to the City of St. Ignace in the state's Upper Peninsula; the principal travel route being state highway M66, a mostly, two-lane gravel road undergoing length stretches of roadway construction improvement, work that imposed numerous tiresome detours, many comprised of risk-taking obstacles; namely, mud holes, large scattered rocks and boulders: the unevenness a constant challenge to our intrepid driver.

We rode in a tan-colored 1934 Chevrolet. The year was 1935 and I was then a tall, skinny, precocious lad of eight. (Please note: At 77, I'm still tall and skinny.) But the memorable utterance my father made at the time was, "When we see milkweed growing alongside this road, we shall know, then, we are in God's country." That observation was the cornerstone of a most remarkable trip under rugged conditions.

With the exception of our, now historic travel difficulties, I repeated my father's remarks to listeners at the Higgins Lake auditorium; and at that juncture, I concluded my speech.

The audience rose to a standing ovation!

Expedition to the North Country
E.P.
November 10, 2004

The following narrative is simply a continuance of my first, youthful, expedition to the primitive North Country. Oddly enough, much of it still is.

It is my recollection that at some point a route was chosen which merged with U.S. 131, another road plagued with construction improvement zones, although all were past our course of travel on what was, now, a paved highway.

Following a night of travel on that awful road previously described, we found ourselves above Petoskey near the west side of large Burt Lake. My dad had learned, earlier, from some factory employees where he worked, to avoid the last 10-mile stretch of highway which was then U.S. 27 (the approximate route of the present U. S. Interstate 75). There would be a line of stalled traffic that long with everyone in those vehicles waiting to board ferryboats for a Straits of Mackinac crossing, they reported.

But a neat trick at hand, the employees continued, was to drive to Cheboygan, located 16 miles southeast of the Straits on U.S. Highway 23. As we discovered, the route was virtually free of any traffic (as it is today!), and we sped to the ferry dock at Mackinaw City where, as foretold, motorists obligingly—perhaps stupidly—permitted our lone car to get in line for the ferry ride. It was, altogether, a cheap, rotten, cheatin' trick, but it sure worked for us – and the temperatures that day must've been in the nineties. It was long before the advent, too, of air-conditioned cars.

Today, numerous, dependable signs posted above interstate routes advise travelers of gas, food and lodging prior to approaching exits. But with the exception of gas, those other amenities were virtually nonexistent in outlying areas during the so-called "Great Depression" era of the 1930s. Gasoline, though, was always plentiful and stations serving it miraculously appeared along roadsides at just the right times; and like today, most cars guzzled gas. Model-T Fords, though, were still in abundance, including other, very outmoded cars, but when somebody drove a vehicle reaching speed of 70 M.P.H. that driver was dubbed "a speed demon!"

Most highway, road or street construction /improvement zones of that era were illuminated at night by spherical shaped metal devices standing about five inches high and served at the top with flat-sided wicks, seemingly made of braided or tough woven cord; and the fuel burned in those lamps was probably a low-grade kerosene, because when lighted, large amounts of black smoke was produced. When spaced at intervals of roughly four to six feet along each side of the work area, the flickering, red-orange glow rendered scenes eerily mindful of the torch lighted flambeau of Hollywood movie horror films.

During our previously described journey to the Straits, a couple of times either my dad or I were obliged to exit the car and do a number one in some roadside thickets. As for mom…well…once we encountered an old, one-room country schoolhouse in decay, but its outdoor privy was still serviceable.

Devotion Versus Combat – A Sad Story
By Edward Pusick

During the American Civil War, a Confederate General – his name was in a history book I no longer have – established a reputation for arriving late on fields of battle with his regiment. The reason for this tardiness was best described by some of his soldiers who said they would observe their commander reading a Holy Bible in his tent. Often kneeling in prayer, his supplications would commence promptly at five every morning, lasting upwards of two hours on most occasions. But it was this religious practice that kept him from responding to urgent appeals for assistance from other field commanders whose armies were engaged in mortal combat with Union forces. However, the day of reckoning was soon at hand.

It was a chance encounter. In the predawn hours of a spring morning, Federal pickets (a scouting screen) were advancing ahead of a long, marching column of infantry comprising several battalions, or nearly 5,000 soldiers, when they met the pickets of smaller opposing force – and the fight was on!

It became a fierce engagement with neither side gaining advantage until the rebels, lacking support, lost the struggle. Meanwhile, all of this occurred within earshot of the featured general of this narrative. Although encamped nearby, and favoring a prayerful vigil, he issued attack orders to his regiment – two hours after the skirmish terminated.

But the man was no coward. At a previous time, when not saying his prayers, the general lead an assault against an entrenched Union detachment. With drawn saber, and brandishing it in a forward motion for his troops to observe, the general guided a charge against the foe, his uniform shredded numerous times by mini balls (rifle bullets).

His military superiors, being cognizant of his bravery were, nonetheless, disappointed with their subordinate's lack of military readiness; and in view of the latest debacle, a decision was made to summon "the reluctant general" to a disciplinary hearing, short of a court-martial.

When brought to that tribunal, it was emphasized that his timely presence during any future conflict with the enemy was of paramount importance; that tardiness due to a religious habit would never again be tolerated, lest he be charged with aiding the enemy.

However, upon receiving this censure, the subject of it complained bitterly, saying: "Dang it all, you don't give me time to say my prayers." And at that juncture, the general explained that Christian prayer was needed to defeat a mostly godless adversary.

At any rate, the reprimanded general took his regiment to a deeply wooded area to await orders for future action. But while waiting there, elements of Union General U. S. Grant's infantry ambushed the rebel general's encampment. It was about 5:00 a.m. when most of his men were asleep. Needless to say, it was a massacre most foul; yet at the start of the melee, one of the raiders discovered the tent of the regiment's commander.

Details are sketchy, but it seems that damn Yankee shot and killed the poor general—as he was saying his prayers!

Chapter 5

Letters from Ed

Those who knew Ed described him as eccentric, witty, warm, personable, perfectionistic, a bit high strung at times, humorous, creative, driven, and in some respects, opinionated. Perhaps there is no better way to taste some of these traits than to read some of Ed's own letters, including those that come from his own remarkable handwriting. Again, a selection of letters was chosen and arranged in chronological order with limited commentary. The first exemplifies his love for local as well as world history:

> Dear -----,
>
> Your phone call before last Easter was a pleasant surprise, made memorable, too, when you introduced subject matter dear to my heart (and intellect); namely, Goguac Lake; and if there is anyone more knowledgeable about the lake than yours truly, then I would like to meet such a person.
>
> My stories and personal recollection of the subject lake might entertain you (and others) for a full afternoon or evening; with these questions, for example, to be raised and answered: Why was the lake named Goguac, and what does it mean? What vast resource was found deep below the bed of it? And in what part

of the lake does a sunken roadway exist? (Discovered when I fell out of a canoe.) Also, where on the lakeshore did an artesian well once flow? It's icy water clean and savory. And last but not least, where near the lake is the stone mansion? Built 66-years ago, but never lived in. Although rarely seen by the public, the elegant structure (rather austere of design yet stylish for its time) remains cloaked with darkly wooded ambience, forever alien to its location: atop an ancient Indian burial mound? The owner/builder died before completing his home's interior…as if the weight of the massive stone-block masonry and slate roofing was already too great for things beneath to bear.

On the chance you will find them interesting—if nothing else, I have taken the liberty to enclose some narratives that address two Goguac Lake incidents of bygone years. These are presented as brief, informal essays of sorts, and you might favor the idea of permitting others to read them, especially those who have their "roots" in Battle Creek.

During the Battle of Britain, the prime minister there, Winston Churchill, gave a famous speech to Parliament in which he said, "I am eager hearted to bring this to a successful conclusion" [meaning the war]. Being of that same persuasion, I am most anxious to conclude this letter…here.

Your pen pal,
Ed
(Handwritten)

Ed also loved to address audiences with his eloquent public speaking skills in addition to his artful illustrations. However, he never referred to himself as an artist – simply a professional illustrator. The following letter pulls back the curtains on one community engagement that was probably replicated in his experiences on many occasions:

October 20, 1978
Wyoming Library Board
Wyoming, MI

Dear [Chair]:

I was delighted to receive your letter of appreciation and, on behalf of Brady, Barnes & Neil, Ltd., my employer, we wish to say we are very pleased to learn the picture, "The Burning Seabird" has been so favorably received by members of the Wyoming Library Board.

On Wednesday, November 8th, I'm scheduled to give a talk at the Wyoming Library. My hour and a half narrative will commence at 7:30 p.m. and my topic will be "An Introduction to Great Lakes Maritime History." During this presentation, I plan to use a large drawing pad on which I will quick sketch some of the important features of different vessels. Today's generation would not be familiar with steamers such as the whalebacks and lumber hookers, yet hundreds of them once plied the waters of the lakes before, and at, the turn of the century.

The authors of books about our lakes' maritime history do not fully explain the nautical terms they frequently employ in their historical accounts. I feel, however, some acquaintance with basic ships nomenclature is essential to the reader's interest. I shall attempt to touch upon some of this informative detail, but as I explain these features, I will illustrate them on the large pad. In this manner, I believe I can hold audience attention much better than saying a lot of things which some may not readily comprehend.

I will also reveal some information not generally known concerning the shipwrecks in our Great Lakes, something which historians perceive will greatly enlighten future generations. But at this time, I feel the little known stories of these ill-fated vessels are as precious as the artifacts they contain. I hope to have present, several of my original works. From the office I can bring the renderings of "The Ghost of the Christmas Tree Ship," a famed schooner lost in Lake Michigan; "The Foundering Lumber-hooker," a steamer which sank three times; "The Doomed Whaleback James P. Colgate," and "The Last Voyage of the Edmund Fitzgerald."

I also hope to have the picture, "Ghosts of the Voyageurs." I may digress a bit during my talk about this scene but I think the information will surprise some of my audience. Last, but not least, we will show "The Bannockburn Phantom," the legendary mystery ship of Lake Superior. The picture is on permanent display at the Kentwood Library.

I would like to add that I don't rate myself an artist and this is not intended to be an art show to promote my work. I'm a professional illustrator and if I use art form, it is delineated and stressed for subject impact. This is what an illustrator is trained to do. Art is secondary here. We want people to start using their libraries and this will be the thrust of my talk.

I don't believe public advertisement of this has been generated yet. ---- said she would attend to this but if you wish you may have copies of this letter distributed to whomever you think will be interested in attending. Whatever information is posted be sure to add that it's for free.

Sincerely,
Edward J. Pusick
(Handwritten)

Even though Ed did not consider himself an artist, this did not stop him from entering his various works in art shows around the region. In this epistle, he described the works he wanted to enter and even gave each his own personal "rating" for each work:

August 15, 1982

To: Michigan Dept. of Education
                 Bureau of Rehabilitation
From: E. Pusick
Subject: Exhibit pieces for Eastbrook Mall Art Gallery Show, scheduled for October 15, 1982

The following list comprises privately-owned pastel renderings of shipwrecks I made (and gave away) which might be considered as possible entries for the show. I am sure that in most instances the owners would be delighted to have them displayed. Those selected should be marked: Private collection – Not to be sold!

Vessel Subject	Owner	Rating
1. Steam barge Jarecki	G. R. Schaffer, D.O.	Outstanding
2. Bulk freighter Bannockbum	Dr. Schaffer	Spooky
picture/story of Grt. Lakes most famous phantom ship.		
3. Wooden freighter Manhattan	R. E. Nichols, D.O.	Eye catching
fire scene.		
4. Steel freighter Noble	Mike McPharlin	Best of my
picture/story vignettes.		
5. Schooner Lydia	Gary Griffin	An arty scene
with sunset which people rave over, but I don't. I prefer action pictures.		
6. Ore boat Clemson	E. Pusick	Small though
especially interesting. Might put a price tag on this one.		
7. Schooner Mars	MI Dept. of Natural Resources	Commission
members considered it to be an outstanding work. It's a very large pastel 19" x 28".		
8. Brigantine Schooner Merchant	U.S. Rep. Hal Sawyer	A good
looking picture/story vignette although there are certain technical flaws in the work – schooners seldom sink by the stern.		

The following pencil drawings might be included with my entries with time permitting. One or more of them might also be printed for a limited edition series.

1. "The Storm Warriors"   Fred Stonehouse   A good action scene of surf line loss of vessel with crewmen being rescued.
2. Propeller Union   E. Pusick   An interesting study with brief historical synopsis.
3. Schooner Lizzie A. Law   E. Pusick   Needs to be reworked but could be outstanding.
4. Schooner Marqette   E. Pusick   A rather good looking study with brief historical synopsis.

Footnote: I have roughed out a sketch for a pastel rendering of the Wallace's Rescue, famous Marquette shipwrecks [sic].
(Typewritten)

At the same time that Ed was showing works in community meetings, art shows, and public institutions, he kept his simple desire to donate works to individuals or businesses to whom he felt endeared. Not being a wealthy man but being a gracious one, he loved to give what he could – his own drawings, or at least copies of them. Here is an interesting case in point:

January 30, 1984
Station Manager
WUOM, 5th Floor, LSA Bdlg.
University of Michigan
Ann Arbor, MI

Dear [Sir]:

I am happy to report that for the past several months I've received the monthly issues of the WUOM/WVGR Program

Guide nearly a week in advance of each new month. Needless to say, the prompt mailing of the Guide *Soundprints* pleases me very much, and in token of my gratitude I've enclosed some miniature souvenir prints of one of my shipwreck studies.

In addition to the print autographed to you, another print is for the receptionist whose courteous reply to my telephoned inquiry last year is remembered. I will appreciate, too, the distribution of the remaining, signed prints to interested members of the WUOM staff, especially to those concerned with the *Soundprints* publication and its circulation.

I do wish I could have included, instead, a check contribution to WUOM/WVGR; shipwreck illustration doing nothing, of course, to support the fine radio programming of your station. My situation as a pensioned, disabled veteran, however, prevents any financial generosities I might otherwise hope to consider in this instance.

In spite of its outward appearance, I am not attempting to advertise my drawing skill. I leave that to a publisher, a noted marine historian, who markets the large, registered reproductions of my illustrated maritime disasters.

I acquire no income from my hobby, but my expenses are covered, and I receive the satisfaction of helping to promote a fascinating subject long overlooked by the general public., i.e., the maritime history of our Great Lakes. Even so, there have been times when I wanted to give free samples of my illustrations to "special" people as well as to friends; hence, I devised the complimentary small print idea.

The prints, however, were not entirely a faithful reproduction. Having been made at a (budget) fast copy center, they will never be recommended as a valuable item for anyone's attic collection. Still, the printed image reflects most of the dramatic action I intended to portray even though its' somewhat darker in tone than my penciled original. The size, too, represents only a slight reduction of the drawing. I plan, later, to make an enlarged master drawing of the scene to accommodate an 18" x 20" limited edition print size. The study will, then, incorporate another vessel, the *Regina*, also lost in the same storm.

Although 11 major lake vessels vanished in the 1913 storm, the *Price* and *Regina* steamers present one of the greatest unsolved mysteries in the annals of Great Lakes shipwrecks. The 12 recovered bodies of crewmen from the *Price* were found wearing lifejackets from the package freighter *Regina*. The *Regina*, however, has never been found!

You will have no need to respond to this letter. I am just an amateur marine illustrator who tends to surface once in a while with rather lengthy letters -- brevity never being one of my virtues. But if I need to express anything more here, it should probably be my sincere hope the "WUOM/WVGR Spring Membership Drive" doesn't flounder!

Vogue la galere,
E. Pusick

P.S. The NPR Playhouse rendition of *Sir Gawain: The Green Knight – Book 5*, apparently, was not aired at the scheduled time last Sunday. Unless I misread my wall clock, or was otherwise confused, it would seem we have a missing "Green Knight" somewhere; then, again, poetry is full of ambiguity. (Typewritten)

As pictured in Chapter 3, it was one of Ed's sketches that graced the cover of a book by Dr. Charles and Jeri Feltner, *Shipwrecks of the Straights of Mackinac,* published in 1991. The following correspondence shows how this friendship began years earlier:

Nov. 26, 1984

Dear Capt. Ed,

What a delightful experience meeting you, finally! Chuck and I sure did enjoy sharing with you at the Great Lakes Shipping Company Restaurant.

Thank you for all the goodies. We do, as usual, really appreciate your thoughtfulness in presenting to us your work. The Severed Schooner, the Blazing Manhattan, the out-of-hand When Things Get Out of Hand, the treasure ship tips, etc. You are a very generous and talented person.

Enclosed is the Xerox copy of The Severed Schooner which you requested, along with a sample copy of the Anchor News (the publication of the Manitowoc Museum.) We are excited about the opportunity for your work to be displayed at the Museum. They are a fine organization, one of the best on the Lakes.

Also enclosed is a copy of Chuck's Shipwreck articles which appeared in Diving Times. I think it would be wonderful if you could make the Sandusky shipwreck come to life. We have no actual photos of this brig, however, it probably looked a lot like the brig pictured in the article.

Take care of yourself, and we'll be in touch soon. I'll send the photos when they are developed. Thanks again for everything!

Most sincerely,
Chuck & Jeri (with permission)
(Typewritten)

Over the years, Ed gave several works to his good friend, Fred Stonehouse. Here is a simple but telling note that accompanied one of those gifts:

12/21/87

> 'Twas a night remembered – "The Wreck of the
> Edmund Fitzgerald." History gets no respect…
> which is why there's such a sad repetition of it.

Dear Fred,

As I don't wish to ship all my eggs in one basket, a second packet of interesting junk will be mailed to you soon. Among other things, it will contain one of my old but recently revised masterpieces of folk art measuring about 8 ½" x 5" image size.

> Keep your anchors aweigh,
> Ed
> (Handwritten)

However, things didn't always gel or come together the way Ed had hoped. On one occasion, sketches that were to go to an author and publishing house didn't arrive in time to go to print. A sense of both disappointment and acceptance can be felt as one reads his attempt to express his feelings:

November 12, 1990 – Veteran's Day
Assistant Director
------- Press

Dear [Madam]:

Granted. My failure to get back to you within a reasonable amount of time is inexcusable. I would hate to think, too, what this delay may be costing your production department. However, the photo slides ---- promised to dispatch to me on Oct. 15 are missing and presumed lost in the mail. A replacement slide which he, later, promised to send me, hasn't shown up yet. The

"Hanging On" illustration, apparently, has failed to hang on, too.

I really don't know what to make of it except ---- is a full-time military career officer whose job now poses grave risks, not only to himself, but to all his unit command subordinates as well, and I'm not about to bug him any further with a problem in the printing arts.

So, it is best that you proceed, immediately, with the publication of ----'s important book, with or without my ol' stuff in it. I'm giving up the ship on this occasion, and regardless of the outcome, you shant receive any future complaint from me.

As always, with sinking feelings,
Ed
(Typewritten)

Occasionally, one of Ed's letters displayed his unique and uncanny ability as a wordsmith, revealing his cultural literacy while at the same time displaying a keen sense of transparency. In his way with words, Ed seemingly attempted to address his own physical challenges with a humorous and euphemistic series of maritime metaphors. Here is an honest message to his good friend, Tom Farnquist:

August 5, 1992
Mr. Tom Farnquist
Commanding Officer
Sea Frontier/Shipwreck Museum
Whitefish Point, Michigan

Ahoy there, Cap'n Tom:

It would be nice to get my leaky flagship underway again, to render more shipwrecking and doodled mayhem; to attack and achieve, perhaps, the ultimate in vehement – though artful – expression; a veritable Gotterdammerung of maritime mishaps and poignant seafaring drama designed especially for your museum needs – and the reference to Wagnerian opera was added here for the sake of erudition. The morbidity of this noble quest, however, does take its strain on things: A short length of mooring hawsers keeps me tied fairly close to the dock!

As the situation stands…or, rather…sits…the ongoing leg-ulcer raids aboard ship have made damage control here a tenuous effort at best, and unless I can repel boarders and put down this mutiny, soon, there's a chance my vessel will sink at dockside – due to rotted hull timbers! Not to worry, though. Because it's better to float than gloat. I intend to be the first one to go over the side following my order to abandon ship; traditional heroics notwithstanding. It's just that I dread to have to command things from a nursing home headquarters.

As always, with sinking feelings,
Ed
(Typewritten)

Ed also liked to write letters of encouragement to his friends and acquaintances. Despite his own skills and expertise, he always seemed aware of the giftedness of those around him, and was not afraid to commend them. And, of course, that was especially true when working together with them on team projects, as the following letter suggests:

September 1, 1992

Dear Colonel Fred:

We in the military should never be taken unawares. Therefore, considering your degree of prowess on the practice field, as well as in the bushes, I'm confident you are cognizant of the impending situation per the (classified) information enclosed.

Unless you are already committed as a volunteer participant in the forthcoming engagement, then I shall recommend (to the Chief-of-Staff) your immediate preparation to move upon their works and summarily: blow them away with your expertise.

Too bad you can't have me there as well. Redundancy is helpful in such matters.

Wishing you the best of success,
Ed
(Typewritten)

Ed seemed to have friends and colleagues everywhere, especially within the military ranks and in high places. Yet, his down-to-earth vocabulary and colorful terms and phrases seemed to season each letter or message. Although his "fighting Illini" friends might not fully appreciate this next letter, it is certainly a delightful read and captures certain of Ed's opinions and personality traits:

Vice Admiral, USBS
Commanding, Sea Frontier, Chief of Readiness
Ninth Shipwreck District (Great Lakes)
September 7. 1992

Dear ---, wherever you are:

Your Valentine's Day letter was a welcome surprise, an auspicious greeting of both enjoyable and informative content; and I especially liked the last (handwritten) notation: "I'll see you in the fall." May that propitious event occur before they haul me away to a nursing home!

It was comforting, though, to learn that you made the grade with your acceptance to the faculty at ol' Grand Valley

U. That's a lot better than having to teach scholarship athletes how to read and write at the University of Ill-n-noids, and institutions of their liberal stripe hand out diplomas to achievers who've accumulated a vocabulary of 150 words or less, including repetitive use of the redundant phrase "you know" in their speech [sic]. We shall exempt, of course, all football athletes from the above critique. Without their play action, life for me would, indeed, be the "pits," and the NFL, too, would be without incoming talent. Ah, yes. Mozart and football is the unbeatable combination for truly great entertainment; and I'm too infirm to play around with women anymore, young or old.

Things haven't gone swimmingly well for me of late although a recent issue of the *Shipwreck Journal* (a quarterly published by the Great Lakes Shipwreck Historical Society) featured a rather interesting profile on me, together with some examples of my work.

Yours,
Ed
(Typewritten)

Mr. Pusick wasn't the best at accepting compliments. But on the other hand, he did feel free to express his disappointment when recognition seemed lacking, or his works were rendered in any fashion that in his mind was less than the best. Here are his thoughts regarding the lasting bronze memorial marker in St. Ignace that bears his own sketch:

October 1, 1994

Ahoy there, Fred:

"Look what they did to my song, ma."
The above, ancient song lyric echoes my dismay upon learning what they did to my illustration (replication). The

enclosed news clipping examples (with photocopy) should afford you the reason for my perturbation.

By all standards of critique, it would be unworthy of me to beat a dead horse here. It's just that it was a total downer to see an attractive image of shipwreck replicated in a [sketch] made difficult to comprehend; not that it's all bad. Devotees of modern art may yet praise the work as a classic piece of ambiguity. Whatever, I can at least be grateful that my name was omitted…!

Lesson learned: Never trust [anyone] to render the work of a "master."

Ever onward…And downward,
Ed

P.S. Well-founded though it may be, the [specifics] of this torpedo missive mustn't be leaked to anyone lest it promotes the small meanness of my character. However, ---- may not escape some measure of my displeasure. He's scheduled to receive one of my infamous shipwreck-doodled Christmas cards. He already knows about those dreadful things.

Ed
(Typewritten)

Ed was not afraid to voice his displeasure, but he always seemed to find a way to lighten the impact with his amazing humor and creative word choices, as this letter to the Director of Housing in Wyoming, Michigan clearly illustrates:

Nov. 4, 1994

Ahoy there,

It's been my long, sad experience to know that most dogs, including those "said" to be friendly, will go ballistic upon seeing me. I suspect the reason is that my metal crutches pose a threat to them; either that or they hate my good looks! Whatever, the black dog which shares the hallways with me here is no exception. Its owner… permits her unleashed pet to roam far ahead of her, a routine that favors my exciting encounters with the enraged beast.

My first memorable meeting with the subject dog occurred during an afternoon last summer when, as witnessed by several other tenants, "El Fido" pinned me against the wall of the (3rd floor) elevator lobby with its arresting behavior. Following seven or so minutes of this harassment, someone there made the wise decision to ask {the owner} to rescue me from her beloved, albeit angry pooch.

The next, and I might say, gripping episode with my worthy opponent took place two weeks ago as I was taking some trash filled bags to the refuse room. The carnivore took that opportunity to make its run on me from astern, permitting only limited time to come about (nautical parlance for turn) and defend myself.

The would-be attacker came in low with lunging, snapping jaws, its bared teeth narrowly missing my ankles. After what seemed an eternity (about 30 seconds), the dog's mistress arrived on the scene—but standing, far off and unobtrusive, seemingly confounded by the situation. I yelled twice at the woman to call the retreat to her engaging pet, and when that failed the desired result, I had to brusquely order [her] to hold her dog until I could effectively manage a get away. And it was soon learned the refuse room was an excellent place to take refuge in.

Although our contests remain scoreless, before my opponent puts any points on the board, it would be greatly appreciated if an arbiter were to referee the dispute. Now it doesn't matter to me, if by HUD rules of definition, the dog has been determined to be small, harmless and suitable for housing here. Unleashed, it might as well be a large attack dog. With that in mind, and considering my vascular leg disorder of long-standing (no pun intended). I reserve the right to demonstrate—as Bill Clinton once did—a measure of honorable cowardice.

Presently, I venture to walk the hallway, or check my mailbox downstairs, at the most favorable time: late at night!

With sinking feelings,
Ed

P.S. As a matter of general interest, the term "El Fido" ascribed to the subject in this letter is an archaic Italian expression meaning The Dog; whereas, the derivative of that is the Latin word Fiduf: referring to the "beloved dog." A good education does serve one well. I might have found a better use for it had I finished high school.

To be sure, not all of Ed's letters were pleasant ones, even when they were intended to be "thank you" messages. The following tidbit shows his penchant for humor that may have trumped or overshadowed the spirit of gratitude that he obviously possessed in this case. There is little doubt, however, that it was taken in stride.

July 10, 1995
TV-5

Ahoy there:

Granted. Your gift of the WNEM TV-5 video: "1913 Storm" was a most thoughtful, generous one – except I don't have a VCR (or whatever it's called) to view it with! That might be a shameful admission: given my profound level of intellect, yet lacking both interest and stipend. Electronic viewing will never become one of my fondest habits, of which there are many. Nonetheless, my vintage black and white, 13-inch (made in China) TV set experiences appreciable usage late at night on certain nights and during the football season; and it never disturbed me when the set's channel selector – permanently lost – lost the channel which carries CBS. It would be perfectly dreadful though if that network decides to televise a number of next season's football games.

But suffice it to say that methods are at hand for putting your video production to good use. A large community room in the (retirement) facility features the equipment necessary for viewing cassette videos and with the management's assistance a showing of yours can be rendered for the benefit of the many seniors living here. Trouble is, most of 'em are old ladies who, by tradition, have a distaste for things nautical – especially shipwrecks.

Ever onward…and downward,
Ed
(Typewritten)

Gratitude was normally something Ed expressed, whether humorously or seriously (though, usually humorously). Perhaps for this reason, it seemed to bother him a bit when gratitude was not expressed. In this particular note of appreciation, Ed hinted at those who never thanked him for his gifts of original art. He also planned to reward the grateful. (This window also discloses his monthly routine of visiting the Veteran's Clinic.)

November 9, 2003

Ahoy there:

Gosh! It was nice to find your letter in my mailbox…like finding a hundred dollar bill on a sidewalk, except with my luck, it would have a picture of Bill Clinton in it!

Still, it would be a most auspicious occasion if we were to encounter each other, soon, at the "dog pound" (Vets Clinic). But here's a reminder: As a rule, I frequent that joint on the 3rd Wed., of every month, between the hours of 10 a.m. and 1:30 p.m., receiving treatment, part of that time, in physically therapy.

My "primitive" pastel rendering of the "Christmas Tree Ship" in your office suite needs my story of that vessel. I prepared it with a small, handcrafted color illustration of the subject, which is featured at the top of the page. When I locate some parchment paper to display the work – and that shan't be anytime soon – I shall require your wife's name. I'm ashamed to say I forgot it; yet, when that is learned, the masterwork is to be autographed with your names.

About a decade ago, at X-Mas time, I mailed a dozen of the above miniature picture/story exhibits to friends (and enemies) of mine. None of them ever responded.

Meanwhile, your letter's enclosure has prompted my response, herein, and it should be a surprise!

I shall resurface,
Ed, Esq.
(Typewritten)

Perhaps the most interesting of Ed's epistles are those that explain some of his works, or how they were inspired or commissioned. In this commentary to a friend, the artist shared the background on a shipwreck illustration he created that adorns both a book cover and a large granite memorial on the shores of Lake Huron at St. Ignace. The work is titled, "What a Way to Go!"

November 10, 2003

"Lord of the Manor:"

Before he retired, Dr. Charles (Chuck) Feltner was the factory boss of the Ford Motor Co., in Dearborn, MI. I, first, became acquainted with his wife, Jeri Baron, when she was both editor and publisher of a scuba diving magazine; and I soon learned the couple were avid divers, noted in the maritime history community for underwater exploration and their discovery of a number of, hitherto, unknown sunken vessel sites in the Straits of Mackinaw.

In 1991, the Feltners authored a book, "Shipwrecks of the Straits of Mackinaw," and they requested that I furnish an illustration of one of their shipwreck discoveries on its cover.

That vessel turned out to be the 2-masted Big Sandusky, which is one of the shipwrecks featured in the news article you sent me. You will find, enclosed, a black and white copy of the finished book cover, although the original drawing – a classic of its kind – is twice the reproduction size; the masterwork presently in the Frederick Stonehouse collection of my work.

And by the way, I entitled my rendition of the Big Sandusky, "What a Way to Go!"

Then, about a decade ago, Jeri Feltner introduced me to a representative of the Michigan Outdoor Writers Association who requested that I forward a suitable copy of the subject illustration. This was needed to replicate an image of the work on a bronze plaque, the latter to be mounted, or affixed, to a huge granite boulder intended for display in a St. Ignace park, commemorating the lost ships, many with all their crews, in the treacherous waters of the Straits.

Following a transfer of the "What a Way to Go" image to a bronze tablet, everything proceeded accordingly. The boulder, with its inscribed plaque, was moved to the dedication site, where, on the appointed day, various state dignitaries and members of the news media gathered....

[By the way], I also reside in a large manor. Except mine is a subsidized housing complex.

C'est la vie,
(so it goes)
Sir Ed
(Typewritten)

Sadly, one of the last presently extant letters written by Ed Pusick was dated December 5, 2005, and sent to a friend in Battle Creek. Perhaps sensing that his life on earth was nearing an end, he typed this autobiographical and historically revealing brief, and began to plant the seeds and lay the groundwork with Lois for the writing of his biography. This present project is a fulfillment of that request.

December 5, 2005
Battle Creek, MI

Ahoy there:

Until the time of my sophomore year (in B.C. High School), my first home was on the western-edge of the city, near Springfield. Then, at various times, I resided with my mother and stepfather at 173 Nelson St., which is located in what was identified as the "Post Addition." In other words, near the Post Cereal Co.

I was seventeen when, in the autumn of 1944, I quit high school to join the U.S. Navy, and it wasn't long before I found myself serving as a seaman on the deck force of a large troop transport ship bound for the North Polar Region via Murmansk, Russia. Following that, I experienced many strange sea odysseys, including a mutiny aboard ship! (An incident our Navy has never revealed…and never shall…for certain reasons.)

Suffice to say, though, I wasn't one of the many mutineers. Surprisingly, they were our ship's passengers: about 2000 U.S. Army Engineering Corps troops, all African Americans: builders of the famed "Burma Road." During their long servitude, which was under hot, jungle conditions, most had taken Burmese women as wives, many having children by them; except the U.S. Army authority refused to recognize these unions; thus, ordering our subject passengers to be returned stateside: without their native families. Consequently, they tried to seize control of the ship, staging an open revolt.

As there were only 460 or so in the ship's crew (including 25 armed, combat experienced U.S. Marines), the situation became tenuous – and I was nearly killed during a mêlée! Yet, fortunately, a number of "key" lower-deck passageways were secured, restricting their use to only ship's personnel needing access to their quarters, crew's mess and the ships' wheelhouse, and the command/communication center: we called it "the bridge."

Meanwhile, the ship's galley (kitchen) and crews' mess: dining compartment, were sealed off so that none of the mutineers could have any food – as it turned out – for the remainder of the voyage to Honolulu, Hawaii. And upon arrival there, hundreds of combat-ready U.S. Marines met us dockside, storming aboard to subdue and arrest the mutineers.

Following my service discharge in the summer of 1946, I enlisted in the U.S. Navy Reserve in 1950, just in time to be called to active duty upon the outbreak of the Korean War. Then, while serving aboard a Navy LST (landing ship tank) vessel, I was injured during heavy seas off "Dead Man's Shoals" (Cape

Hatteras) – a storm that nearly sank the LST. But after being taken ashore, I was declared physically unfit for future duty; subsequently, receiving an honorable discharge. Nonetheless, my eligibility to receive certain medical benefits was approved; namely, medicine: pain killer issued at the pharmacy of the local VA Outpatient Clinic, a facility I call "The Dog Pound!"

You will find, enclosed, a photo of my lovely, loyal companion, Lois, together with a view of Tom Farnquist, director/curator of the Shipwreck Museum at Whitefish Point, MI. Herself, a published author, Lois is preparing my biography.

C'est la vie (that's life: how things happen)
Ed
(Typewritten)

Chapter 6

Letters to Ed

Many letters to Ed were left behind among his personal effects. Some were from military officers, some from publishers and authors, and others were from museums, libraries or institutions to which Ed graciously donated his works. And, of course, some of these letters were personal. Contents from a few of these have been selected to give the reader a window into the generosity and personality of Mr. Pusick.

On the 2nd of August, 1978, Ed received a thank you from the Officer in Charge of the Grand Haven Coast Guard Station. The letter simply stated:

> We would like to extend our deepest appreciation to you for the painting you have donated to our Station. The painting dramatically portrays, in the highest traditions of the Coast Guard, the humanitarian purpose to which we and our fellow Coast Guardsmen have dedicated ourselves down through the years. Those who have viewed it have noted that it instills a deep sense of personal pride and satisfaction in our work; causing us to further dedicate ourselves to upholding the noble traditions of the Coast Guard.

Again we would like to thank you for sharing your time and talents with us. (Typewritten)
A color photo of the picture as displayed was also included with this message.

Ed felt strongly about preserving the history of the Great Lakes shipwrecks within the body of Michigan's maritime heritage. For this reason, he tried numerous avenues and publication venues to include his works. Some materialized, others did not. Here is an example of one from a maritime press dated September 28, 1978 that did not yield the results Ed had hoped for:

Dear Mr. Pusick,

I've been sorry about not being able to help with your very worth-while and long-needed project on Great Lakes shipwrecks that should be preserved as you are endeavoring to accomplish. Keep up the good work! Perhaps, one of these days, I'll be of some use. Please feel free to call on me for aid any time.

I appreciated receiving the photo proofs, and I am looking forward to seeing the series of proofs that you mention in your letter.

Congratulations on a very laudatory contribution to Great Lakes history.
(Typewritten)

While some doors closed for Ed, others seemed to always be opening. Many of these were from community organizations that sensed a connection with the man behind the art. This message from the Wyoming MI Library Board on September 27, 1978 serves as an example:

Dear Mr. Pusick, Illustrator,

The Wyoming Library Board is very excited over the presentation of your original pastel entitled "The Burning Seabird." Our thanks go to you and to your company, Brady, Barnes and Neil for this lovely gift.

The story of the Seabird was not known to any of the board members, and we feel that by sharing it with us and with our community in such a unique way that you have brought alive a part of our Michigan history to all of us. We would welcome information concerning the other Great Lakes disasters you are illustrating to share with our library users.

Thank you so much for making our Wyoming Library a more beautiful and interesting place to visit. (Typewritten)

Some of the correspondence revealed that Ed also did some public speaking and presentations as part of his quest to disseminate Michigan's shipwreck history. On September 7, 1978, he delivered a speech at Higgins Lake during a commission-sponsored meeting of the State of Michigan Department of Natural Resources. A note on this letter explains that Ed's speech was tape-recorded, and when he finished speaking, "the audience – about 400 in number – broke into loud, heavy applause [Ed]" (Pusick, handwritten).

Dear Mr. Pusick:

On behalf of the Natural Resources Commission I would like to thank you personally, and the firm of Brady, Barnes and Neil, Ltd., for your gift to the Department of the original pastel rendering titled "The Wreck on South Fox Island."

We enjoyed your presentation to the Commission on September 7, at Higgins Lake. While in the Director's office this week, I had an opportunity to view your work which is currently displayed in his office. This is unquestionably an

outstanding work of art, and one that this Department shall cherish. The portrayals and history of the events you depict are among Michigan's most valuable natural resources. Again, our many thanks for this gift.
(Typewritten)

Another benefactor of Ed's work was Michigan State University. A chain of correspondence shows the bit of a challenge Ed navigated, but in the end, the university was a grateful recipient.

February 27, 1979

Dear Mr. Pusick:

I've spent a little time tracking down correspondence, notes, etc., to establish where we are with respect to your donation of a pastel rendering to Michigan State University. I have developed the following course of action.

First, it appears that your donation would receive maximum visibility in our Library, Kresge Art Center, or The Museum. Thus, I am forwarding a copy of your letter of February 21, 1979, to the directors of each along with a brief explanatory note in which I ask them to get in touch with you directly if they would be interested in receiving your donation. If more than one contacts you, I suppose you will have to choose which will receive the rendering. I have listed appropriate contact persons in the event you need to communicate with them.

Should you not hear from these individuals within a reasonable time period, I'd be happy to become involved once again.

Finally, this department would happily accept your rendering, but I feel it deserves the wider visibility offered by the other units mentioned. (Typewritten)

Less than a month later, Ed received this follow-up letter from Michigan State University:

March 22, 1979

Dear Mr. Pusick:

We have received information regarding your proposed donation of a pastel rendering of a lumber ship. Our Curator of Exhibits is currently preparing a traveling exhibit on Great Lakes shipping which will include models and illustrations of ships. This will be loaned for short periods to museums and other appropriate institutions in the state. He tells me he is also planning an exhibit on Great Lakes ships for our museum in which he may be able to use your illustration. [Mr. Pusick's handwritten note here indicates, "Acceptance Action OK'd."]

We would be happy to consider adding your pastel to our collections subject to the same conditions under which we accept any donation. The museum staff must be able to make the final decisions as to how, when and where the object will be exhibited. We cannot guarantee that all items donated will be forever on exhibit, although we do try to put each new donation on exhibit for at least a short period of time after it comes in. It may then go into storage for use in an appropriate exhibit at some later time. We have many things in storage but we are constantly drawing from those collections to create new exhibits so that there is always something new for the public to see.

If these conditions are acceptable to you and you wish to donate your pastel to our museum, I would be pleased to hear from you.

Sincerely,
Curator of Historical Artifacts
(Typewritten)

[Mr. Pusick's handwritten notation adds: "Museum acceptance of donation approved by phone, per curator of artifacts, Mar. 26, 1979. Rec'd my O.K. for travel exhibit, but on loan basis only. E.P."]

Further correspondence a month later explains how the pastel was formally accepted, a recognition plate was engraved, and a special ceremony launched its display in MSU's "Natural Resources Building." Evidently, the artist was quite pleased.

But it seems quite evident that not all of Ed's donated artwork went to institutions. He also gave his sketches, pastels, or paintings to lawyers, business owners, and community members who showed an interest in Ed's passion for maritime history. One Grand Rapids lawyer wrote on September 16, 1982:

Dear Ed:

I wish to thank you for the print of the "Smith Moore" which you gave to me. I am certainly pleased with the picture and it is now hanging in my office for all to see.

I certainly enjoyed speaking with you on September 15 and would like to have lunch in the near future so that we might discuss some of your many adventures. Again, thank you so much for the print; it was most thoughtful of you.

Yours very truly, … (Typewritten)

On occasion, Mr. Pusick contributed a work of shipwreck art not only to an organization, but to a specific member or officer within the organization who engaged in diving among these very shipwrecks. The following letter was addressed to one such individual who experienced a dive to the John M. Osborn, and who was a member of the Crooked Tree Arts Council of Petoskey MI. (Today, Mr. Ley serves as the Development Officer for the Great Lakes Shipwreck Historical Society.)

May 5, 1987

Dear Ed:

Please accept this letter as my most sincere personal thanks for sending me your beautiful print of the JOHN M. OSBORN....

As soon as I can, I am going to frame the print and hang it in a very visible spot in my office here at the Arts Center in Petoskey. It is truly something I am proud of: because I was able to dive the OSBORN myself and because you gave it to me personally.

Ed, I have been a musician all of my life and am just now taking my first drawing class at the Arts Center, to try and demystify the creative process of visual art in my own eyes. It is a real challenge, but has provided me with a lot of rewards even this far.

The Great Lakes Shipwreck Historical Society is the most worthwhile project-organization I have seen in a long time. It is to the Society's credit that you and I were able to meet. There is a possibility that I can involve your work in our Gallery or our Art Tree Sales shop ... and I'll talk to you about that the next time we meet, which I am sure will be sometime this summer at Whitefish Point.

In the meantime, take care of yourself; you have a valuable talent that the Society and its members and visitors need.

Yours most truly,
Sean Ley [with permission]
(Typewritten)

Of course, not all letters that Ed received or sent pertained to his art. A letter he received from the Michigan Bureau of History on July 26, 1988 humorously reveals his perfectionistic tendencies:

Dear Mr. Pusick:

Thank you for your recent letter concerning our mathematical error on the back cover of the May/June 1988 Michigan History magazine. We appreciate your sharp eye and your interest in Michigan history.

We hope you enjoyed the article on Charles Lindbergh's Michigan connections in the July/August 1988 issue.

Sincerely, ...
Publications Assistant
Bureau of History (Typewritten)

Ed's perfectionism served him well. It was because of this pursuit of excellence that several authors trusted him to illustrate their writings in periodicals and books. One author from Iowa wrote this update on October 13, 1989.

Dear Ed:

Please forgive my delay in getting you these copies, but everything I have written the last three years suddenly ended up on my desk in the last two months for revisions. I also started teaching for the first time in 10 years, and had to give a speech at the maritime history convention in Toledo, and then got sick, and the result was that I went a little bananas. Hope these copies are not too late to be of any use to you.

I'll also send you the details of a heavy weather-winter costume described in an 1890 autobiography: "When on deck on a cold stormy night, I would wear a pair of light cotton stockings, a light pair of sheepskin moccasins, over these a pair of heavy Canadian stockings that reached over my knees, and a pair of high-topped rubber boots; also a one-piece suit of underwear, a suit of heavy Canadian underwear, a heavy blue woolen shirt, a pair of serviceable thick trousers, a heavy double—breasted pea—jacket, a long oilskin, and knitted skull cap and sou'wester with heavy leather belt made fast around me." Unfortunately, there are no pictures of this get-up. You will see that most of the Xeroxes may not help you much. Iowa has a huge collection of costume books, and I looked through them all to get these. I wish I could have been more help. If I run across anything in 19th century magazines--sometimes there are illustrations--I'll copy it and send it along to you. Hope all this helps.

Talked to my editor and she was crazy about your drawings. She may yet put one on the cover; she is still deciding between that and an historic painting. Even if she decides for the painting, I would love to use one of your drawings on the cover of the next book. Thanks again for allowing me to use them; they are some of the most beautiful drawings I have ever seen. And it won't hurt to be known by the senior editor of the University of Michigan Press.

Hope you are keeping well. I saw Fred at the convention in Toledo and he said that you had gone to the dive for the Fitzgerald. Glad you could get away and I hope it was enjoyable.

I still owe you lots of favors. If there is anything I can do for you in the way of research while I'm here this winter, let me know. If not, I'll see you next spring when I come north.

Thanks again so much for allowing me to use your work. I really appreciate it and your drawings made the book a lot nicer than it would have been otherwise.

Yours, … (Typewritten)

Remarkably, Ed's works were also featured September 12, 1999, on the History Channel in a special documentary on "Shipwrecks of the Great Lakes" within the series, "The Wrath of God." Here is both the letter and the release for that telecast from Tower Productions of Chicago:

May 25, 1999

Dear Edward Pusick:

Thank you for sending the print of the Edmund Fitzgerald. Fred Stonehouse sent me the other print I requested. Your work is remarkable.

I have included a standard release for your signature. Please, sign and mail back to me at your earliest convenience. Contact me with any questions.... I appreciate your wonderful assistance with this documentary for The History Channel.

Sincerely, ...
Associate Producer (Typewritten)

LETTER OF AGREEMENT FOR USE OF STILL IMAGES

Date: May 25, 1999
Re: Agreement with Edward Pusick. [Mr. Pusick's notation: "These illustrations were showcased Sept. 12, 1999 on the History Channel. E.P."]
To: Edward Pusick
          Marine Artist/Illustrator

This is in reference to the material described below:

(2) Illustrations titled, "They Lost the Struggle" and "Don't Allow Nobody on Deck!"

This letter will confirm our agreement with you Edward Pusick that in consideration of screen credit, Edward Pusick will provide the above—described material for inclusion in an episode of The History Channel's series Wrath of God tentatively entitled "Shipwrecks on the Great Lakes," and hereby grants to Towers

Productions, Inc. the non-exclusive right to use this material in the aforementioned episode for distribution as follows:

In standard television, non-standard television, and videogram throughout the world in perpetuity (see attached definitions).

Your signature below will warrant and represent that you own the copyright in the above described material and that you have the authority to grant the rights, as described above.

If the foregoing is acceptable to you, please so indicate by executing and promptly returning to us the enclosed copies of this letter, in which event it will become a binding and irrevocable grant and license. _(Agreed to and Accepted)_____ [Signed by Ed Pusick]_____ (Typewritten documents)

Thankfully, Ed did not see his works' TV debut as the ultimate accomplishment to the point where he stopped donating his works to local settings. And, as a veteran of the U.S. Navy, he continued to feel a bond with the Department of Veterans Affairs Medical Center in his hometown of Battle Creek.

June 16, 2000

Dear Mr. Pusick:

On behalf of the Battle Creek VA Medical Center and the Grand Rapids Community Based Outpatient Clinic, we wish to offer our sincere gratitude and appreciation for your recent donation to our Community and Volunteer Service program by providing artwork. The artwork will be a wonderful addition to the Physical Therapy suite at the Clinic. The artwork is being framed and will be hung in the near future.

Donations such as this are always needed and definitely appreciated by our veterans. It's so important for them to know that they are remembered by those in the community, and your kind donation certainly conveys that message to them. Thank you for your support and continued interest in the welfare of our veterans.

The Battle Creek VA Medical Center or the Grand Rapids Community Based Outpatient Clinic did not provide the donor any goods or services in consideration in whole or in part for the above contribution.

Sincerely, ... (Typewritten)

Occasionally, Ed's artwork ended up in the most uncanny places, and not through his own initiative! The following letter tells of a special and unusual location of Ed's work that will not even be seen for years to come:

21 June 2004
Mr. Edward Pusick

Dear Sir:

Before I forget it I want to tell you about an unusual place where your outstanding artwork lays! Several years ago the citizens of Mackinaw City decided it was time they 'planted' a time capsule containing documents and history of the Village and Area. A suitable site was selected at the North East corner of the Village Cemetery, close to the rail fence. A Village crew excavated the hole and a gigantic coffin-like receptacle was readied with a waterproof lid.

The High School Band attended, songs were sung, speeches made, etc. I had been asked to contribute something about diving in the Straits area – but fortunately I thought of Chuck and Jeri Feltner's grand book on that very subject! I phoned Jeri and she made arrangements for me to go to Shepler's Marina Store and pick up a copy which she and Doctor Feltner would donate to the project. I got the book and delivered it to the pit attendant at the ceremony.

When the great container was sealed and the hole back-filled, the Village crew built a sidewalk leading to a gigantic stone they placed over the spot. I believe there is now a bronze plaque on the stone telling of the time capsule beneath and giving a date for it to be opened. YOUR BEAUTIFUL COVER ARTWORK IS ENSHRINED there for years to come!

That's all the time I have today – making the week-long preparations to leave for Mackinaw next week. I'll keep in touch.

Most sincerely, ("YOURS, AYE!")
Captain Frederick Leete III [now deceased]
U.S. Coast Guard Licensed Master
Master Instructor
Command Diving Officer (Typed)

Finally, it has always been one of Ed's wishes to see his limited edition shipwreck prints on display throughout Michigan's shores in the many historic lighthouses. For this reason, the present authors have personally delivered prints of the Edmund Fitzgerald to lighthouses in Escanaba, Traverse City, Mission Point, Port Huron, Bay City, and Ludington. The following letter selected for this chapter indicates the beginning of this legacy during Ed's own lifetime:

FORTY MILE POINT LIGHTHOUSE
Rogers City, MI 49779

October 26, 2004
Mr. Edward Pusick

Hi Ed,

How is everything with you? I'm sorry I haven't written sooner, but I'm still catching up on paperwork from the summer.

I am enclosing a picture of your framed pictures as they are displayed in the lighthouse museum. This is the second picture we took…. I hope you can tell that we've framed each B&W picture with grey and white and used metal frames. The one colored picture is similarly framed; however, we used a blue to make the picture stand out better. The pictures are always a big hit with our visitors. They are a great asset to our museum. Again, thank you for them.

It was a pleasure to see you in August. I was very surprised, to say the least. Tell Lois we said hello and I enjoyed reading her book.

Yours truly,
Barb Stone [with permission]
(Typewritten)

Lois with Ed at Whitefish Point

Ed presenting his limited edition *Edmund Fitzgerald in Storm* print to Captain Leete

Chapter 7

Reflections of a Caregiver and Personal Tribute

When Lois joined Ed on that trip to Whitefish Point in the Fall of 2005 to deliver limited edition prints of "Don't Allow Nobody on Deck" to the Museum, the two of them first searched for Captain Leete's lake cottage in Mackinac City to hand deliver this rare print. (It was later learned that Captain Leete donated his prized, rare print of "The Fitz" to the Mariners Church in Detroit where he said it would have greater visibility.)

After a delightful conversation with both the Captain and his wife, Ed and Lois enjoyed a pleasant and delicious lunch while Lois watched with amusement as both Ed and Capt. Leete vied for being the first to tell their tall tales from their old seafaring days. With lively animation they also discussed their conflicting theories of how "the Fitz" sank. The following is Lois' account of that memorable trip and other reflections:

*   *   *

Arriving at The Great Lakes Shipwreck Museum at Whitefish Point, the Executive Director, Tom Farnquist, took us on a pleasurable tour of the museum where he gave us an inside glimpse, showing findings from many of his diving expeditions. Later, we checked into our motel in the tiny town of Paradise then Tom came by and took us out to eat at a quaint restaurant known for their whitefish. He treated us to an exquisite meal and played the gracious host, having known Ed for many years and wanting to show his appreciation for all of the many original shipwreck drawings Ed had bestowed on him through the years.

The next morning we drove along the picturesque coast in the Lower Peninsula to Rogers City. Again we were treated like "royalty" at the 40 Mile Point Lighthouse, which was a mostly red-brick, two-story structure dating back to 1897. Ed wrote, "Although its light remains operable, being maintained by the U.S. coast Guard, the building was donated a number of years ago to Presque Isle Country for use as a maritime museum; and included in its display of nautical artifacts, is a large, invaluable collection of some of my rarest limited edition prints of historic Great Lakes Shipwrecks; scenes as they might have been witnessed, three of them featuring highly unusual picture/story exhibit prints of mine." Each one was tastefully framed and gracefully lined the walls of this old but beautiful lighthouse.

It was at this juncture that we made the acquaintance of Barb Stone, the secretary of the "Society" that contributed volunteer work on the lighthouse restoration, and renovation. Ed had only known her through many years of correspondence so they were delighted to finally meet in person.

We sat on an outdoor bench while being served a delightful cup of coffee. From there we were offered a close view of a windy, blue Lake Huron with its rock-strewn, wave-tossed beach; "altogether a bracing unforgettable sight for us," as Ed wrote later.

Barb connected us with Denny Moran who later that evening guided us to the local town pride, their new Masonic Temple. Ed wrote,

> It seems a majority of men-folk residents are Master Masons, many of them former lake sailors, while some still work on the "lake boats," as they are, affectionately, called. Needless to say,

the latter is a misnomer; the definition being that any vessel large enough to carry a boat (aboard) should be called a "ship."

At Denny's suggestion, Lois drove us to a sizeable downtown restaurant of lighthouses and lake vessels. The surprise, though, was the huge pizza served to us. Expressed as a medium size pizza on the menu—what would a large one be?—it was the likes of which neither Lois nor I had ever previously enjoyed.

This pizza's most notable feature was that it was covered with a rare brand of hauntingly tasteful olive oil, making it literally, a "wet, delicious pizza." Topped with black olives, red bell peppers, onions and hamburger, "the piece d occasion" (meaning: piece for a special occasion) was its mozzarella cheese topping which, upon eating, stretched to foot-long strands, a noble characteristic denoting authenticity; whereas, imitation mozzarella will not display the marvelous phenomena.

How I [Lois] Got To Know Ed

If I had to give a description of Ed in one sentence I would have to say that there really wasn't a category to totally describe how engaging he was to those that had the fortune to meet him. When I think of him I automatically get a smile on my face and a warm feeling in my heart. His speech not only was peppered with eloquent phrasing but one could usually expect a sly dry wit interwoven and almost hidden among each of his meticulously chosen words.

Thinking back to that first day in 1998, I recalled a lanky frame supported by specially made candy cane shaped crutches meeting me at the door of his upstairs apartment in the small city of Wyoming, Michigan. He greeted me warmly and invited me into his tiny but cluttered living room hobbling past to clear a space on the well-worn sofa, or davenport as he called it.

My line of work had been Home Health Care for quite some time. I encountered many interesting people through the years, helping the very rich to the very poor, the very sick to those who just needed a little help to get through their day, and high maintenance individuals along with those who appreciated the smallest task I did for them.

Although my main reason for visiting Ed was not for entertainment or enjoyment but to help with some daily activities that he found difficult to do with his present leg affliction and arthritis, I found myself looking forward to my bi-weekly visits.

Soon we became friends. I found myself hanging onto every word he said as I busily did his chores around his tiny dwelling. There was no endless patter but rich history lessons, delightful anecdotes, and witty sayings. I also was able to glean stories from his childhood and learned much about his background. The ardent notes I took along with many of Ed's writings hopefully give the reader a glimpse into his personality and remarkable life.

With anticipation Ed looked forward to our weekly endeavors, usually going grocery shopping then having lunch afterwards. The following letter written to me on June 18, 2003 not only showed his sense of humor but also his almost childlike delight with the simple things of life:

Dear Lois,

It should be noted there was never a need to complete this letter before now. That's because the effort required my deepest concentration and thought to prepare its unique sentence structure: the product of a brilliant mind. And if you believe that gobbledygook, you'll believe anything.

I "savored the rare and precious card" you sent me, including your note [inside]; and your kind, thoughtful remarks launched an idea concerning our next luncheon. Given an agreed upon date, I believe it would be a nice change of pace to alter our venue by having our noonday conference and lunch at one of my favorite eateries: the Big Boy restaurant in Rogers Plaza.

If you haven't discovered it, the cuisine at Big Boy is delectable; and I suggest you try their "gangster-style" spaghetti with meat sauce: the latter seasoned with garlic, basil and oregano. It's especially delicious, though, when the hot, naked, oiled pasta is first layered with melted mozzarella cheese; and a dish of this high caliber is rarely enjoyed outside of Chicago, or New York.

Unfortunately, many were the gangsters who were shot to death by members of rival gangs as they dined on Sicilian pasta dishes, such as described.

But not to worry! There won't be any "contract out" for us, and you shan't be hit with paying the tab, either. Meanwhile … "here's looking at you kid."

Ed, Esq.
(Handwritten)

Another letter dated November 5, 2004 Ed wrote:

Dear Lois, "lady of swamp things!"

Your name should be changed to Lola. No, I've not lost my marbles—just gained some. Anyhow, like the lyrics of that old song: "Whatever Lola wants Lola gets," you seem to get what you want: like some of my money every week. On the other hand, you've been a reliable chauffeur and helper—better looking than George, too.

But what I need from you, at this time, are answers to the following questions:

1) What was the date of my pastel presentation (and speech) at the DNR auditorium? I guessed it was Sept. 10, 1978. I seem to recall one of the DNR commissioners by the name of Pridgeon sent me a thank-you letter, copies of which you have.
2) Does your husband, Gary, have a PhD? There's a reason for this question.

Anyway, my exuberance carried me away, last week, at the Meijer store, but I've since returned to earth. Meijer doesn't feature the deli sale item I often crave that Family Fare does; namely, whole fried chicken, or even fried chicken pieces.

The following suggestion is a concept of my "beautiful mind": The day before Thanksgiving, let's feast on Boston Market roast turkey, dressing and other goodies purchased at that store. However, you will first need to procure a copy of the Boston Market menu.

And lest I forget, please source a black (or blue) book cover-binder for the stationary you bought for me: A Knight of Arms—and crutches too.

Sir Ed
(Handwritten)

Living on a limited budget Ed had to be careful what he spent. He relied on his Social Security check each month with that being the only income he received, thus explaining why he had to live in a government subsidized apartment. Unfortunately he never received disability payment from the Navy. His explanation of this was rather vague – something to the effect that his referral physician reviewing the casework took a disliking to him and altered the records.

George, a man in his latter 60's (and referred to in several of his letters) was employed by the apartment complex to drive, for a low cost, some of the residents to their doctor's appointments and errands. George was a real joy to have around with most residents appreciating the extra work he did to make their life a little easier. The following note illustrates some of the rapport he had with Ed:

I surmise it was you, George, who left the package of delicious "Brach's coffee flavored toffee candies on my front door. Regrettably, though, I cannot pay you for the fine gesture until my Social Security check is posted at the bank on the 3rd of next month.

However, if you encounter my ol' pal and travel companion Lois Hauck, before then, I am confident she will be happy to reimburse your expense ($3 dollars or so), on my behalf, for the aforesaid candy.

Then another note that came to me showing the teasing relationship they had after Ed had accidentally left an article in George's car:

You need to make a comeback to George's mean-spirited remark about you and he awaits your response. Therefore, you might tell him something similar (in vein) to the following, except put it in writing so that I may pass it along.

You are not running a taxi service for Westwood Apartment tenants; hence, you are not responsible for any articles Ed might leave behind. Then, too, you are neither a paid escort nor Ed's babysitter! But there's something else you can use for verbal ammunition. Recently, George (believe it or not) mistook you for someone else. You could really have some fun with that dumb faux pas. At least tell George that he's getting very old and senile when he can't remember a pretty lady's face.

Eccentricity

I [Lois] recall a unique and very specific task that Ed had me do the moment I arrived at his apartment one day. After our usual greetings followed by the sound of his crutches scraping the door as it slid shut, he seemed unusually agitated but got right down to the point. "Lois, I need you to find my special razor that I haven't seen in ages!" That led to questions about what happened to the one he used every day and where should I start looking for this appliance. It wasn't as if I had many rooms to search and certainly I should be able to come up with the lost item in no time.

I looked in drawers, cabinets, closets, and even an old beat up suitcase stashed in a corner bedroom but to no avail. Ed continued wringing his hands, moaning and groaning. Around 30 minutes had passed when he suggested, "Why don't you look in my fishing tackle box." Trying to suppress a smile I asked, "Now why would it be in there?" Only silence came with that question.

But to find the tackle box! Fortunately I didn't have to look very long and did find it located inside a small filing cabinet. I pried open the rusty latch as the top layer sprung open revealing a mismatched collection of old lures, hooks, lost buttons, safety pins, corroded batteries, etc. Pulling out the bottom tray I saw a small box that I almost shoved aside but he told me to open it. There nestled under some tissue paper was the lost "antique" razor. Even though I had been looking for it for some time, I was surprised and intrigued why and how it got in the tackle box.

Ed had the answer on the tip of his tongue when I asked how he thought it ended up there. "I hid it there in case I had an intruder and he decided to be greedy!" Yet, I was rather amazed that he would even think of hiding it there. He was normally so careful about personal items staying clean that he even had me wash his plastic cutlery before throwing it away!

His unconventional behavior carried over into his personal achievements. While others admired and cherished his shipwreck drawings, very neatly printed stories, and numerous letters, of which he had made copies, there were many days that I found these items carelessly thrown in the garbage can in the corner of his drawing room. Thinking that maybe he used the can as a storage bin for these rolled up treasures, I suggested that we should put them in a safer place. "Leave my trash alone! It's rubbish and not something that anyone in their right mind would want!"

I somehow convinced him that these were works of art that should be admired by others. Even the letters and notes were artful since most had very tiny and neat printing plus some of his famous doodles on the top. Soon he began shoving these kinds of items in my hands saying, "These are for that 'Museum of Oddities' you insist on having!"

One of the notes I found described Ed's thoughts about a cleaning lady that worked for him in the 90's. It read:

> My introduction to Pat Dean came at a time most needed. Her mother-in-law, Gertrude (and also my neighbor) was

aware that I suffered – it was during much of the 1990's – with lengthy bouts of Venous Stasis Ulcers on my left lower leg; being cognizant, too, of my need for domestic assistance: i.e., a housekeeper and laundress, Pat Dean was to fill that void at rates I could afford, and Pat occasionally would shop in retail stores for me, continuing her faithful service until a few years ago. (Typewritten)

In her own tribute to Ed, Pat recently shared, "Ed was a quiet man who never wanted any praise for any of his drawings. He wrote beautiful stories and was a wonderful man with a big heart, appreciating everything I did for him" (phone conversation, March 13, 2013).

Ed loved it when I dropped a card or note in the mailbox. Even though I saw him in person twice a week, he still enjoyed hearing from me in that way. He also delighted in returning a letter or note that usually was carefully worded and fun to read.

Dear Lois,

Now that both of us are becoming famous, there is no reason to share the limelight. This is due to the desperate nature of our skills, not social standing.

First, you are expected to require handsome residuals from the sale of your new book, whereas my reward claims only the adoration of a single fan, namely Capt. Leete.

But rather than go our separate ways, I suggest the following solution to this dilemma: exchange your SUV for a stretch limousine, preferable a black Lincoln model with dark-tinted windows; the limo to feature a luxurious, commodious interior, complete with reclining seats, a small fridge, TV set and music (Bose radio) sound system. Champagne served with delicious canapés will be the norm.

In anticipation of this, you are expected to wear a chauffeur's uniform complete with cap and drive the limo whilst I entertain lovely female guests in the passenger compartment. Your daughter, Heidi, is expected to be one of them!

Signed, Ed
(Handwritten)

A letter addressed to me and dated 10/16/04 made reference to one of the nicknames I had for Ed:

Dear Lois, "Lady of the Rogue River swamp!"

I need you, your family needs you and the following warning is issued in order to preserve your safety and sanity:

Recently, when your slip-of-the-tongue revealed that you had returned to the dangerous sport of "Roller Blading," I was simply aghast and dismayed. Will you never learn? Such wild behavior could lead to a more serious injury than the broken wrist you suffered while skating: like a broken neck!

From now on, I shan't turn off my phone ringer at night in case Gary should call with some dreadful news about you.

Forever yours,
"Mr. Ed"

P.S. I still insist the real Mr. Ed of TV comedy fame was a mule rather than a horse. Therefore, please check the truth of the matter at a local public library. Librarians do keep trivia information about such things and will be happy to share it with you. In retrospect, though, I'm really not keen about sharing a name calling with either a horse or mule. (Handwritten)

Occasionally I got "accused" unjustly, but it usually was in such a teasing manner that I didn't mind. A letter written to me on November 28, 2003 demonstrated such a case:

Dear Lois "Havok"; a.k.a. the Turkey Bandit!

For a long time I pondered the wisdom of posting the enclosed letter. After all my critique of you smacks of overkill. But fun and games—and insults aside—where would I find another good ol' buddy such as you… my adopted daughter, too?

Your recent sleight-o-hand trick demonstrates an adroitness in deception worthy of a magician's skill. I refer to the turkey caper you successfully pulled off on me.

Last Thanksgiving Day, as I prepared to enjoy a sumptuous dinner comprised, mainly, of several leftover slices of (Boston Market) roast turkey, much to my surprise—and dismay—I discovered they were not in my refrigerator.

It seems that when you were here, last Wednesday, you, somehow made off with the turkey (literally, under my nose) without attracting my attention.

The regrettable consequence of the loss was that I was obliged to dine on some leftover stuffing layered with turkey flavored gravy, served with remnants of jellied cranberry sauce. There was nothing left for me to savor, except bitter thoughts.

Therefore, Lois, you continue to create havoc in my state of affairs; yet if I accept the excuse that your removal of the subject (turkey) from my abode was entirely accidental, then I would sooner believe the notion that turkeys, like chickens, have teeth!

Taken for more than a ride,

Ed

P.S. For our outing, next Wednesday, I believe George should be invited to join us. He would keep a sharper eye on you than I could; thus, preventing you from causing further trouble … for now, that is. (Handwritten)

After receiving his letter I gave him a call to suggest that maybe he didn't look hard enough in the refrigerator. Sure enough, there on the right shelf towards the front but under one of his side dishes, and much to his delight, he found the container full of leftover turkey.

But in a letter dated a whole year later (12/18/03) he was still referring to this incident:

L.L

You should be so lucky! This being the season to be jolly, you are getting a fasting reprieve. I discovered a Mountain Jack's $4 off (luncheon for two) coupon. If we go there, next month that is, I shall dine on a delicious prime rib with all of the trimmings, whilst you may enjoy a large tossed salad (sans dressing) with the usual black coffee and a glass of water. You will be served bread, of course, but without the butter.

But first, on X-Mas Eve, I want you to go to Boston Market—my finances permitting—and purchase the same ala carte turkey slices (serves-3-4 people) which you enjoyed last Thanksgiving. There should also be plentiful sides to order, such as stuffing with gravy. But this time, you will not be able to make off with the turkey! (Handwritten)

A letter dated February 11, 2005 reflected on my news about losing one of my clients due to having to be placed into a nursing facility:

Dear Lois Lane,

You poor thing! For years, you toiled diligently as a reporter for the Globe, a local newspaper; employment that paid you a weekly wage amounting to peanuts—yet, they were always fresh roasted ones. Nevertheless, it is unfortunate to learn you have since been laid off, except you might recall some of your pleasurable job benefits: such as the time I rescued you from the clutches of that evildoer, Lex Luthor; and those thrilling moments we shared, speeding together through the upper atmosphere… breaking the sound barrier.

Meanwhile, the advent of extensive cell phone usage has made telephone booths, virtually obsolete. For that reason, I change clothes now in the toilet stalls of public restrooms, and in those reserved for women only, my wardrobe change is rendered with the speed of light, but not so fast as to prevent me from looking around, so to speak. Recently, though, my ol' nemesis, Luther, tried to contaminate me with some poisonous Kriptonite, a powerful allergen which he knows my system cannot tolerate. It produces a catatonic state of mind; wherein, I become, both mentally and physically an infant! But not to worry. A return trip to the planet Mars refurbished my extraordinary powers.

Your faithful Superman
AKA: Clark Kent
(Handwritten)

- -

Please separate this form from letter along dashed line. Check appropriate box and return to sender:

__ Yes, you will be my Valentine
__ No, you will not be my Valentine
__ You are undecided
__ None of the above

One of the cards that I sent him had a heavy set lady in an old-fashioned bathing suit complete with ruffles and a cap pictured on the front. On December 12, 2003 he cut the front cover off the card and wrote the following on the back:

Lois, "Lady of the Lake"

The card you sent made me think of you so much that I've decided to return it's cover. The ruffle [on the suit] doesn't make a difference, either.

During our next restaurant outing, I plan to order just a glass of water, a cup of black coffee and two slices of dry, whole-wheat toast for you. After all, I have your health to consider— and think of the money I'll save, too.

Ed

(Handwritten)

A card of apology was delivered to my house one day after Ed had not been his usual cheerful self during our errands. I honestly thought his behavior wasn't nearly as bad as that of some of my clients and didn't give it a second thought.

To Lois Lane, my "Lady of the Lake":

Without your continued friendship (and companionship) there would be nothing left to live for. But knowing that I deeply offended you during our last outing—by my cursing histrionics—please accept this as my formal apology. Such misconduct of mine was entirely reprehensible, and now I endure shame and regret. Even so, I beg your forgiveness!

[Upon opening the card I noticed he had drawn a dog with a very sad face.]

But you can't really say that I'm in the doghouse because of what I did. I live in a large kennel, and you know where that is.

The good news is that I'm receiving distemper shots now. So it will be safe for you to pet me again. (Handwritten, February 21, 2004)

Another witty letter from him was sent shortly after Valentines Day in 2003:

Dear Lois,

Gosh! It was mighty thoughtful of you to remember me with a St. Valentines Day card. You might've received a homemade Valentine from me—and it would've been exceptional—except for the fact I spent too much time developing a big Valentine for my lovely girlfriend, Stephanie, who works in the Wyoming Housing office. And, yes, like Cupid's arrow, my Valentine scored a bulls-eye! But there's no point in revealing what she did for me.

Meanwhile, "come up and see me sometime." But since time is needed for an orderly scheduling of my future, numerous dates—a lot of women visit me—a four to five day advance notice would be greatly appreciated.

"Here's looking at you, kid!"

Ed, Esq.

P.S. The lengthy cold, snowy weather prevents me from reaching a barber shop, so I look pretty much like this, now: [He drew a funny caricature of what he must look like with long hair.] (Handwritten)

Since Ed lived in government subsidized housing, there were many different challenges to face on a regular basis due to unruly neighbors. One such neighbor had gone on a rampage threatening to kill everyone in sight. He had gone off his medication that should have been taken for his condition. A reference to this occurrence was in one of his notes to me dated January 12, 2004:

L.L.

Be sure to mark your calendar for our next important business/luncheon date on the 21st of this month. We will dine on gangster-style spaghetti at the Big Boy restaurant, but in case

I'm short on cash, you shall have the pleasure of watching me eat. Your coffee and water will be optional.

And since you continually mention Antonio in your communiques, when he returns from Pine Rest I will see that you have the opportunity to meet him.

He can be expected to go after you in a big way!

Pleasant dreams,

Ed

(Handwritten)

Being a worrywart, Ed could carry on for days about things that were totally out of his hands. Most of these were minor issues so usually I tried to spare him from information that would cause any unnecessary anxiety. However he tormented himself for weeks upon hearing that the housing authority was going to have to rewire his apartment and update his kitchen. I received this letter from Ed after I suggested that we could go on a "field trip" of some sort to get him out of their way:

Good ol' buddy Lois:

The more I think about it, the more it appeals to me. I refer to your earlier suggestion that we visit Battle Creek (and the historic sites of my youth there) on one of the three days of my kitchen make over: Sept. 17-19. I would prefer Fri., the 19th to be the date of our (archaeological) expedition since I have yet to procure another means of escape from my apartment that day, but I shall have to settle for whatever you decide.

Nonetheless, all of your expenses will be paid for the trip; and there's a delightful, old-time cafeteria in B.C. where the food served puts Old Country Buffet cuisine to shame.

Ed

(Handwritten, August 25, 2003)

Before our trip to Battle Creek, Ed sent me this request:

Lois,

Ask Gary if he will join us on our next exploratory expedition to Battle Creek. It would be nice if he could share our interest in the (actual) historic sites of my early youth and, then with time permitting, we might reach Dr. Vince's Island to see if any ruins of his great house remain there. It was destroyed by fire in 1966, yet with luck, remnants of that mansion might invite your examination and give you the opportunity to photograph them. In such case, I shall take the precaution to remain in the safety of your car. "The Hound of Baskerville" could very well be on the loose in that dark, brooding locale. I refer, of course, to the killer dog in the Sherlock Holmes mystery story.

But fanciful tale aside, we must repair to Shrank's Cafeteria for a much needed delicious repast; and we can introduce Gary to some of [the] restaurant's calves liver, and mac and cheese cuisine.

Ed, Esq.

P.S. My knighthood is pending, and when that is bestowed on me, I can be addressed as "Sir Ed." (Handwritten)

We did make this eventful trip. The whole experience seemed to delight Ed so much that he was almost childlike with his exclamations over how things had changed and how others seemed to look the same. Stories were pouring from his lips and told with such eloquence that on the way home I hardly remember driving.

A letter dated the following week (October 8, 2003) stated:

Dear Lois—formerly, "The Lady of the Lake"

There could be a restoration of your grand title provided certain (watery?) tasks are fulfilled. But first, please find enclosed my check reimbursement for your purchase of film and photo development.

And now on to ancient legends and that "Holy Grail" stuff:

That we failed to find the haunted mansion built atop an ancient Indian burial mound on one of the Goguac Lake Islands only raises new questions. For example, if Dr. Vince's great house was destroyed in a fire (circa 1966), it's remains might still be evident, provided the site is accessible; and who knows what precious artifacts these may invite our examination.

Yet, if we were to mount an archeological expedition to [that] island in the future, then it should be timed during a season when heavy foliage will not obstruct our view.

I shall, of course, finance the expedition (our second quest for the Holy Grail) with fifty bucks going to you with all meals furnished, including our return visit to historic Shrank's Cafeteria for a delectable repast; and with luck, perhaps pig hocks with sauerkraut, a longtime staple there, will be featured on the menu.

And as that great English author, Rudyard Kipling, expressed it, "Once more to the breech dear friends, once more to the breech." At my age of 76, it's fun to be a bit disoriented; and here's to our next field adventure in Battle Creek.

Cordially yours,
Ed, Esq.
Knighthood pending
(Handwritten)

Then another note:

Dear Lois,

For faithful service, above and beyond the call of duty, you are hereby awarded the enclosed bonus (check) payment of $25.00.

I shall keep a record of this—pending your next merit rating review. But should your work effort prove to be unsatisfactory in the future, you can be assured the above amount will be promptly deducted from your wages; assuming, of course, you are still my employee.

Sincerely,

"Ebenezzer" Ed

P.S. Unfortunately I owe you for a car wash. Perhaps, though, we can negotiate a fee amicable to us. Meanwhile, I trust you not to divulge any of this to the I.R.S. (Handwritten)

A letter dating October 18, 2003 made reference to this return trip to Battle Creek:

Dear Lois, "Lady of the Lake" and groundwater, too!

I propose that we spend part of our business meeting next Wednesday (the 22nd) dining at the Big Boy restaurant in Roger's Plaza. There we can enjoy some of that delectable gangster-style spaghetti again, which will be at my expense.

Upon our return here, it would be an auspicious occasion if I were to have the opportunity to introduce you to "Babe" (second in command of this joint). She and her boyfriend—if you recall—assisted me on my first archaeological expedition to Battle Creek, exploring many of those historic sites there which I've chronicled and –with perseverance—shall make famous! At any rate, Babe will learn of your invaluable expeditionary assistance to me; that we plan a return visit to [B.C.] to photograph the legendary "water park" of my early youth, and with luck, examine the ruins, or site, of Dr. Vince's (enchanted island) great house.

And with time permitting, we can exhume some, if not all, of the ancient art supplies and rare drafting instruments: relics of past endeavors stored in my bedroom, all to be given to your son, Andrew, a future architect of what will be of a Frank Lloyd Wright caliber, or near that. Years ago, in Chicago, I was "schooled" by a student disciple of that great building designer. And having run out of space here, there's only this small space left to sign off:

Ed, Esq.
(Handwritten)

Another office employee was a favorite of Ed's. Of course he had a tendency to favor only the female workers. He sent me a picture of her with this note:

The young woman pictured with me works in the office here; and because I never had one of my own, I regard her as my adopted daughter! And having bonded, we often chat—on company time, so to speak. This affords me the opportunity to lend her some fatherly advice. For example, my "daughter" wears a small, silver ring in her navel, but I've convinced her that she must replace it with a large diamond, like the one the popular songstress, Britney Spears, displays in her belly button. Important things of this nature should be of concern to any caring father. (Handwritten)

For some unknown reason, it seemed like most of Ed's correspondence to me involved food. Of course that was a matter of most importance to both of us. I even had someone once say to me, "Lois, food is important to you, isn't it!" after I had exclaimed several times over my meal saying how good it was. After that remark I noticed that she never commented on how she liked her food.

January 9, 2005

Dear Lois:

We must forego our adolescent fantasies and return to reality. You are not Lois Lane and I am not Superman, although I'm a lot smarter than he is.

In the effort to curtail my excessive spending habit, I plan to remain in my lair, next Wednesday. For that reason, you may have to go to either Pizza Hut or Culvers for our noonday sustenance. However, I tend to favor the latter. My food order there would be "Kraut dogs." My burger—not to be overcooked—should be served with mustard, ketchup, pickle and onion; and I suggest you try one of their kraut dogs, too. You, of course, shall be reimbursed for the expense, together with your (usual) visitation fee.

And should you encounter George, during your visit, remind him that when he used to drive me around, the physical activity kept him trim and in good shape. But since you've taken over the duty of being my chauffeur, his (obese) figure has gone to pot!

Obviously, the Post Office was unable to sell the swamp creature stamps I so envy. It's a pity that I failed to buy more when they were available. Perhaps, though, some of the horror movie monsters will go on sale. I could always use stamps featuring my favorite movie star, "Frankenstein!"

From a beautiful mind,
Ed
(Handwritten)

Continuing to pit George against me (in a teasing manner) he wrote the following on February 4, 2005:

Dear Lois,

Your good name and character have been impugned; so, it's time that you retaliate with proper action: go to your battle stations, immediately!

Last Thursday, during the early afternoon, I encountered George (your ol' nemesis) in the downstairs front lobby. The area was crowded with residents, some with relatives and friends, all hearing the nasty, mean-spirited things [he] said with a loud voice, about you; all stopping their conversation to listen, some in quizzical dismay, others responding with amusement.

Addressing me, George made this "foul" statement: "Lois paid $1200 to have her rear-end differential fixed, but ask her if the repair work was for her car?"

Second insult: "Lois is old ... claims to be 53. Her brother, though—the one she never knew—must've been killed during the 1st World War!"

I swear the above quotations to be true, and with true patriotic tradition, "Remember the Alamo, Remember the Main and Remember Pearl Harbor," get even with George for demeaning you, moreover in public, in such a dire, vicious, low-down fashion.

Your champion and militant supporter,

Ed

(Handwritten)

His Last Days

Nothing could prepare me for what I was to face one day when I came to his apartment. The day seemed like any other day.

As I punched in his apartment number at the entry door below to wait for him to buzz me in, nothing happened. I punched it in again. Still nothing.

One of the women from the office saw me and arose from her desk to come and let me in.

"How are you today?" she greeted me smiling then added, "I wonder what that old rascal will be up to today."

When I didn't respond with a comical retort but told her of my concern that something just didn't seem "right," she agreed and said that she hoped everything was okay when I got to his apartment.

The old elevator seemed to take longer than usual to reach the first floor. In fact, it seemed to be stuck. So I gave up waiting and climbed the stairs to his apartment. I headed down the long narrow hallway and knocked on his door, still wondering why he wasn't there with the door propped open with his crutches. There was no response so I knocked again and shouted his name. Still nothing!

I could hear my heart pounding in my ears as I made my way back down the hallway to the stairs. I headed to the office to ask if they could come upstairs with me and let me in knowing I wasn't going to find anything pleasant.

The office lady asked me to hold on for a moment while she finished what she was doing, then opened the drawer for a master key and arose from her chair to follow me back to his apartment. She repeated what I had done, first knocking then calling out his name.

The key rattled in the doorway and when we opened it -- there he was, lying on his back on the floor in front of his drafting table. It was a kind of natural pose as if he had just laid down to rest on the floor, although I knew he would never have done that, knowing he wouldn't be able to get back up.

I rushed over to him calling out his name with no response from him. I shook him, called his name again, and then felt his pulse. He was still warm but I couldn't get any vital signs so I had the office call 911 for me as I began CPR.

I continued doing this as the dispatcher coached me through words given to the office lady, but to no avail. I knew it was too late. He was gone.

Before I knew it, I was sadly attending the funeral at Fort Custer in Battle Creek.

*　*　*

Knowing Ed personally was a blessing. His humor, creativity, eccentric personality and spirit of friendship were personally enriching. And he inspired all around him with his love of history and strong sense of patriotism.

Ed always attracted much attention when we went on our outings. Not only did he draw attention from his height with his lean figure leaning on his odd shaped metal crutches but he always wore a baseball cap that had both WW2 and Korean War on it. Not too many individuals could claim to have served in both wars. I was proud to be seen with him and hear what people had to say as they thanked him for his service. We were often waiting for the doctor at the Veteran's Facility (which he called the Dog Pound) when I heard many of the fascinating stories about his life, service and his amazing creativity. These became added to the record that I amassed.

Following Ed's death and very meager memorial service, my goals became to give Ed the tribute he deserves by preserving his story and preserving his works. My husband, Gary, helped me to achieve the first goal by assisting in the compilation and writing of this project, and the second by establishing the Ed Pusick Gallery in the Instruction North Building of Montcalm Community College in Sidney, Michigan, where Gary serves as the Dean of Instruction. The gallery is filled with many of Ed's discarded works that I salvaged, in addition to many works that he gave to me and my family. It also includes his drafting table, instruments, a collage of his life-story, and early original drawings. The subsequent chapter gives reflections of art instructors and students of Ed's many works housed there and included in this compilation.

Above: Lois presenting a Pusick limited-edition print to the Flat River Historical Museum (President Bill Garlick and Vice President Carolyn Garlick); Gary at Ed's marker on the shore of Lake Huron at St. Ignace by the Straits of Mackinac; Below: Stephanie Hamilton and Mollie Boutell exploring the Ed Pusick Gallery on the campus of Montcalm Community College in Sidney, Michigan.

Chapter 8

The Legacy Continues

During these years since Ed's death, we have spent many hours going through the scores of drawings, prints, notes, writings, letters, and other written artifacts that Ed Pusick left behind. These have now been donated to Montcalm Community College to establish the Ed Pusick Gallery in the Instruction North Building on the main campus in Sidney, Michigan. The writing of this narrative and compilation of these works is the fulfillment of a commitment that Lois made to Ed. His legacy endures, and his life and works continue to inspire us, personally.

We have continued the quest to deliver limited edition Shipwreck Prints to lighthouses and museums across the state, and have visited many historical maritime sites in the process. These visits encompassed several shipwreck sites, including those of the *Nahant* near Escanaba (Lake Michigan west shore), the *Bermuda*, *Herman Hettler*, and *Scow* near Munising (Lake Superior), the *William Young* near St. Ignace (Lake Huron), and the *Duval* sister-ship near Ludington (Lake Michigan east shore). We have also explored the museums of the Great Lakes from Manitowoc to Escanaba, Traverse City to Bay City, Ludington to St. Ignace, and Munising to Port Huron. And we've visited sites from the Davidson Shipyards to the Mariner's Church, which resides next to the waterway connecting Lake St. Clair (and upper Great Lakes) to Lake Erie.

Most importantly, we carry the memories and thoughts of a man whose passion it was to preserve the heritage behind these sites, and promote a deeper understanding of the brave men and women who sacrificed all in the pursuit of maritime commerce on our Great Lakes. It is our sincere hope and desire that the disseminated and displayed works of Mr. Pusick will both educate and inspire many for years to come.

The Ed Pusick Gallery

Replete with Ed's drawing table, instruments, letters, awards, books, pictures, drawings, sketches, paintings, architectural sketches and portfolio, the Ed Pusick Gallery is open to students and the general public during normal business hours September through May, and has free admission. One of the regular uses of the gallery is to provide an avenue of study for students of visual arts at Montcalm Community College. Collegiate artists of varying ages analyze and reflect on Mr. Pusick's works to sharpen their own skills of illustration. Many are asked to muse on these works in the process. Here are just a few of many art student reflections.

Sydney Hedrick writes:

> Edward Pusick has a very clear, realistic style. Each one of his works shows an immense amount of detail. I find it wonderful to see just how much detail can be found in pencil drawings. I was drawn to three particular drawings, *They Lost the Struggle, It Wasn't a Good Day for a Trip on the Lake,* and *When Things Get Out of Hand.* Each one of these pictures depicted tremendous amounts of detail, value, proportion, and movement. The range from dark to light truly shows the realistic nature of the waves. It's incredible to me to see sketches like these and from a first glance, not be able to tell if they were photographs or not. He

really puts you in the middle of the action. The gray color scheme gives each picture a mellow mood, which provides contrast from the subject of each work. (Hedrick)

Kristine Mangus adds, "His art provokes an instant sense of wicked, relentless fury on the high seas [as the Great Lakes were often called]" (Mangus).

Contrasting Ed's shipwreck drawings with his more comical illustrations, Barbara Garvon comments, "As I first looked at his drawings, the subject matter seemed so dark and tragic. But I've also seen the funnier side of his works. His illustrations are so exceptional! What a love he most have had for the Great Lakes and all his subjects" (Garvon).

Michael De La Fuente likes Ed's unique initials that resemble a ship. To him, they resemble Ed's own sketch of the Aurania, bearing the two distinct masts. "The Aurania sketch looks so realistic – almost like a picture of the real boat" (De La Fuente).

Several students landed on a particular sketch or drawing that was of particular interest. Talisa Bergeron gives the following commentary on *They Lost the Struggle:*

This piece of art is very well done. It has a great use of shading and many details in it from the violent waves to the articles on the boat. It creates an immediate mood of fear and sadness with the graphic portrayal of sailors struggling for their lives and drowning. Even the remarkable shading of the sky clearly conveys the intensity of the weather. (Bergeron)

Elaborating further on *They Lost the Struggle* along with *It Wasn't a Good Day for a Trip on the Lake,* Jace Sweet adds:

Ed Pusick's illustrations of maritime disasters struck a chord with me, especially those pieces showing the incidents *in process.* His detail and balance almost bring the moment to life.

In viewing *They Lost the Struggle,* (and *When Things Get Out of Hand*), you can almost hear the voices, the shouts of urgency, and despair.

In *It Wasn't a Good Day for a Trip on the Lake,* the men's faces exhibit both resolve and sorrow as they struggle with the waves to escape the disaster. But they seem reluctant to abandon the ship that has carried them safely so many times before. (Sweet)

Several also commented on the *Blazing Manhattan.* Chaley Harris observes, "The penciled waves are amazingly life-like! If I didn't know it was a drawing, I would certainly believe it was a photograph. Incredible! I also found Ed's accompanying story beautifully written" (Harris).

And Sarin Hoogeveen adds, "The *Blazing Manhattan* also uses a variety of textures with dark and light shadows to add depth and intricate detail. Each line, shape, and cloud of mist helps to graphically tell the story, in addition to adding variety and balance to the drawing" (Hoogeveen).

Others saw similar detail with the *John M. Osborn.* As noted by Ryan Jensen, "The values in this piece are amazing. It also looks just like a black and white photograph! The waves are crafted beautifully. The artfully drawn smoke stands out against the clouds and sky in the background, and his use of space is excellent" (Jensen). Travis Ogle adds, "The waves, sky and smoke are all convincingly realistic! I am impressed with what can be so well portrayed using a simple pencil" (Ogle).

Lost to the Gale also draws numerous reflections. "This work truly casts a wave of emotion over me," confesses Amber Mogg. "The contrasting subjects of nature's rage with man's courage create a hurricane of thoughts for anyone who sees it" (Mogg). Stephanie Hamilton agrees, and calls it "a very suspenseful drawing." She continues:

There are very dark shadows and lines that exaggerate the drawing. You can see the meanness and heaviness of the waves. Pusick also portrays a very dark sky, which is to me, an angry sky. The people in the row boat seem to be in panic. He shows this by dark shading and the value of the people. There is very little white value in this drawing. The waves are intricately defined and dominant as they take over the boats. (Hamilton)

Ed's drawing, *When Things Get Out of Hand* always generates interest as well. Mackenzie Paulen notes how it "shows the absolute strength of the water, and the power it has over the ship and its crew. In an ironic twist of fate, it demonstrates how the water and ship work together in its obvious, impending demise" (Paulen). Emily Walsh views this work not only as depicting an historic event, but also a metaphor for life. "As the rough waters beat against the ship, four people can be spotted paddling away from the ship. From this drawing I feel the message is clear. When things get too rough, sometimes you need to get away" (Walsh). Randi Veltkamp concurs that maybe hope for those survivors is the true subject of the work:

> This drawing is of a large sailboat that is blowing over in a raging wind storm. In the background you can see a small rowboat with four people inside, evidently escaping the sinking ship. Using carefully detailed shadowing, Ed Pusick showed how violent and deadly the storm had become. However, in the background the sky seems lighter where possible hope may be for the sailors who escaped. (Veltkamp)

Yet another favorite is *Steamer on the Reef,* drawing similar observations. "*Steamer on the Reef* is a line drawing that uses many values of light," writes Logann Liebrock. "It clearly captures the essence of the story that accompanies it. Leaving the helpless boat, frantic crewmen are escaping on lifeboats to an arriving tug. The attention to detail is amazing" (Liebrock). "The rough seas are portrayed so realistically," adds Jared Wierde. "You can almost feel and hear the waves crashing over the boat" (Wierde). Robert Hill agrees, "I like the realism of the drawing. The water looks like it is flowing on the page! It even strikes

some fear in me as though I was on that boat as a member of the crew"
(Hill). Elizabeth Cornelisse expounds:

> The *Steamer on the Reef* is a picture of a steamer in the
> middle of a storm. The ship is ready to sink and the crew is
> rowing away in a lifeboat. You can almost feel the turbulent
> water just by looking at the picture. The ocean is very angry
> looking and I can imagine the fright of the crew in the tiny
> life boat.
>
> The focal point of the picture is of the large steamer itself.
> It is that which first captures your eyes. Second, you notice the
> small lifeboat beside it. The picture uses a mixture of values
> from light to dark. Even though he uses a wide range of value,
> the whole picture seems dark because of the disaster he is
> portraying. It is such a vivid piece." (Cornelisse)

Of course, the *Edmund Fitzgerald* always garners much attention
in what is perhaps Ed's most famous work, *"Don't allow nobody on
deck!"* According to Pusick's brief description below this title, this was,
"Reportedly, the off-mike order of Captain Ernest McSorley to his
crew during the late afternoon of November 10, 1975. The admonition
was overheard by the pilot of another vessel in radio contact with the
Edmund Fitzgerald" (Pusick). This amazing blue-tinted drawing is a
"2005 Special, Limited Edition Commemorative Print."

"This is truly a masterpiece," muses Andrew Wucher. "The precision
of detail and use of curved lines graphically represent the movement of
the ship. I used this as a topic in my Communications Class" (Wucher).
"And the waves are crazy!" adds Melissa Brainard. "I feel like someone
is about to fall off the ship! With his use of line and value, one can feel
the texture of the waves" (Brainard). Ironically, what captured the eye
of Taylor Rish was the uncanny appearance of the clouds. "They look
so real," Rish states. "The value of the clouds stirs you with the feel of
the storm" (Rish). Taylor visited the Shipwreck Museum at Whitefish
Point and remembered the story of "the Fitz."

Katlin Hopkins also visited the Shipwreck Museum before this study experience at MCC's Pusick Gallery. She chose to reflect on the work that combines the *Edmund Fitzgerald* with the *John M. Osborn*. She shares:

> As a little girl, I would go with my family every year to the Upper Peninsula. We saw several ships during these trips. I remember hearing about the *Edmund Fitzgerald* and picturing it in my head. (I have been to the Whitefish Point Shipwreck Museum as a child, and it became one of my favorites.) Interestingly, Mr. Pusick's illustration exactly fits the description I was given and remembered. I particularly liked the drawing that compared the *Edmund Fitzgerald* with the *John M. Osborn with barge tow.* The drawing captured how each of these ships was distinct. One can also feel the rolling waves surrounding the *Fitzgerald,* and the gentle currents in the setting of the *Osborn.* In both cases you can see the texture of the water. (Hopkins)

Commenting on the same work combining these two ships, Carrie Kaat adds, "He uses a lot of shadowing in both drawings, yet there is a subtle difference between the two. He really captures the unique nature of both ships and their settings. They show what painstaking attention to detail an artist must give to illustrate well" (Kaat).

Shane VanPatten chose to study a work of Mr. Pusick, which to the best of anyone's knowledge, was never sold or published. The original piece is in the Ed Pusick Gallery, and shows the section of the Edmund Fitzgerald's bridge in which the captain's helm was located. The setting is obviously on that tragic day of November 10, 1975, and was drawn by Mr. Pusick on October 10, 1990 as a "suggested (flawed) study." Ed based this drawing on a photograph taken of the sunken vessel during a dive that he personally attended. He called it, "The Surprise! – Sudden sounding of the Edmund Fitzgerald." (The photograph can be found on the cover of *The Great Lakes Guide to Sunken Ships* by Karl E. Heden, published in 1993.)

The Surprise !
Sudden sounding of the Edmund Fitzgerald
— A suggested (flewed) study by : Ed Pusick 10-10-90

Van Patten writes:

> This drawing is showing me how the ship was being beaten
> by the violent waves, pounding against it from every side. Water
> was splashing and pouring onto the boat at an alarming rate. It
> only shows the letters, "D Fitzgerald," and the drawing is not
> straight. It is offset to add character and powerfully portray the
> power of the storm. There are two crew members on the ship,
> and their behavior is striking. What must be going through
> their minds? Is this the end? (Van Patten)

And then, there are the other non-ship works by Pusick, also on
display in the Gallery – most of which are originals. Some are simple
doodles, and others may have been attempts for publication. One
popular sketch is, "The Investigator," which Ed identified as "Visual
subject matter for *Remarkable Riddles of the Great Lakes.*" As discussed
earlier, the illustration is of the skeletal remains of an officer from the

shipwrecked *Alpena*. When discovered in the sand dunes, the hand was still clutching the hat.

Jeremy Hill writes of this piece,

> This picture reminds me that life is not guaranteed. We all eventually die. Some will die young, some old, and some middle-aged. Some will die painfully while others die peacefully. None of us knows how or when our lives will end. To me, the skeleton in the drawing represents the unknown…. Maybe this is why this work is called, "The Investigator." (Hill)

Referring to a similar piece, Katrina Nelson explains,

> Ed Pusick's artwork is a variation of literal marine pencil scenes, cartoons, and a few morbid scenes. I especially liked a skull that he drew in pencil. The focal point appears to be at the nose, very dark. In fact, other than the eye sockets (which seem to be crossing comically), it is the darkest object on the page. His use of shading makes his compositions seem like they are about to come to life on the paper. I fully expected the skull to start bouncing and open its jaw as though speaking.

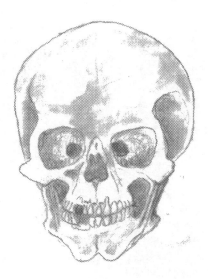

His style seems relaxed to me, regardless of the piece. It is always very clear what Mr. Pusick wanted to convey to his audience. From turbulent waters to amorous bunnies, his work is complete and appropriately detailed. (Nelson)

One of Ed's pencil doodles on exhibit is "Child in Wagon w/ Flashlight." Ryan Flowers was enamored with this piece because, as he explains, "I have two trouble-maker boys and I can see one of them performing this action!" The drawing shows a child going down a hill in a wagon at night using a simple flashlight. Ryan continues, "Ed nicely captured the action of the moment, the path on which the wagon was rolling, and the sense of imminent danger. The message to me is that children, or maybe all of us, may attempt to do some dangerous things in life that take us down some troublesome journeys, while holding onto what makes us feel safe" (Flowers). Interestingly, Ed explained that while in Jamaica he personally experienced seeing the local children precariously careening down the mountainside in their crude, handmade wagons.

Another captivating drawing is simply titled, "Oops!" It graphically shows a man with an axe kneeling over a body. Marissa Netzley suggests, "Even in this simple doodle, Ed's use of line and texture makes the scene come alive." But, Marissa does not view the axe-man as an accidental murderer:

> I see him as a family man chopping down wood to warm his house, or a lumberjack coming home from work. To me it looks like he stumbled over the body or happened to walk by. His axe has no blood on it and the body looks like it's been there a while. Even the face on the man carrying the axe looks more like, "What is this doing here?" rather than, "What did I do?" Of such is the detail of Mr. Pusick's works. (Netzley)

Oops!

And Marissa is exactly correct. According to Fred Stonehouse:

> The story ... starts with the loss of the steamer John Owen on November 13, 1919. The 281-foot, 2,127-ton composite

steamer was downbound from Duluth with wheat when she sank in a terrific gale, taking her entire crew of 21 men and one woman down with her. The location of the sinking was never determined, but was thought to have been somewhere northwest of Whitefish Point.

The following March, a Coast Guardsman running the mail with a dog sled team discovered a body frozen in the shore ice to the west of Crisp's Point. After great effort, the remains of the man, later identified as the Owen's assistant engineer William J. Reilly, was chopped out of the ice. Loaded on a sled, the body was returned to the station and stored frozen until instructions regarding its disposition came from the Lake Carriers' Association. The body was in excellent condition, except for two missing fingers supposedly accidentally chopped off when the body was being freed from the ice. (Stonehouse, *Haunted Lakes* 140-141)

Several art students related works of Mr. Pusick to their own experiences either in life or career. Danielle Tryastad liked the "Sketch of an Aging Man." She explains:

> Being a nurse, I always find myself staring at my older patients wondering who they "were." I wonder about the things they've been through, the lives they lived, and most importantly, the knowledge they hold.
>
> This picture has small, simple details that tell a story -- the coarseness of the nose hair, the shading around the lenses (to emphasize the thickness of his glasses), and the contouring of the lines that shape his increasing wrinkles and aging skin. The artist also played to the physical changes of the enlargement of the ears and nose that come with age. I imagine this man to have been a serviceman who still appreciates the simple pleasures in life. (Tryastad)

Molly Boutell enjoyed Ed's sketch of his "Caribbean Office," or "Busy Office Complex," as he liked calling the open-air seaside bar in Jamaica where he did his drawings over a few drinks in September of 1985. She shares, "I like the relaxed irony of this piece. Although Ed is supposedly busy about his drawings while talking with the bartender, the setting of the beach and gentle movements of the birds and a stray cat add to the sense of repose in this sunset scene" (Boutell).

For many students, Ed's works bring warm and soothing feelings, either associated with the subject matter, or memories stirred by his art. Jessica Adams recounts, "His drawings remind me of a wonderful time I experienced a couple of years ago when my Grandma took me to explore the Upper Peninsula and the shipping locks of Sault Ste. Marie" (Adams).

Ed's legacy also continues in the hearts of so many with whom he associated during his illustrious career. Sean Ley, Development Officer of the Great Lakes Shipwreck Historical Society reflects, "Ed so impressed me as a very cordial, polite, and wonderful man. He and I loved to chat about his artwork. Perhaps the most interesting feature of working with him were his little 'vignette' drawings that he would include in various locations, just for fun" (Ley, 20 Feb. 2013).

Divers and authors Dr. Charles and Jeri Feltner add their tribute:

> Ed Pusick, Captain Ed, as we always called him, was truly a wonderful, kind, caring and considerate person who gave his all to his friends - from his heart to his hand that carried the utensils that created his masterpieces of shipwreck drawings. He conveyed so much of his feelings and his knowledge of those ships through writings that he did on the many prints of his drawings he generously gave to us. We were deeply honored when he agreed to do the shipwreck illustration for the cover of our book *Shipwrecks of the Straits of Mackinac*. We were blessed with his friendship and will always remember him with deep appreciation, respect and gratitude.
> Jeri Baron Feltner and Dr. Charles E. Feltner, March 14, 2013 (Feltner email).

All in all, it is incontrovertible that Ed left behind a rich legacy of life perspectives through his illustrations, letters, writings, and the memories he produced. The Spring/Summer 2006 edition of *Shipwreck Journal* aptly stated:

> Ed's artwork … was truly prolific. Ed was a quiet man, a bachelor all his life, whose passion was his artwork…. Ed was the source of many inventive designs as a professional, but apparently never took the trouble to seek patents, recognition, nor much gratitude for his work…. While Ed is gone, and we will indeed miss him – his spirit lives on forever in the works of art he created for all of us.

Works Cited

A Maritime Press. Letter to Ed Pusick. 28 Sep. 1978. Typewritten.

Adams, Jessica. Unpublished essay. Montcalm CC., 21 Jan. 2013. Handwritten.

"An Excursion to Tragedy." *Shipwreck Journal.* Spring 1998: 1, 3. Print.

Bell, Debbie. "Ed Pusick's Art is Filled with Both Tragedy and Humor." Unpublished reflections. Montcalm CC Art Department, 21 Jan. 2013. Handwritten.

Bergeron, Talisa. Unpublished essay. Montcalm CC., 25 Jan. 2013. Handwritten.

Boutell, Molly. Unpublished essay. Montcalm CC., 21 Jan. 2013. Handwritten.

Brainard, Melissa. Unpublished essay. Montcalm CC., 21 Jan. 2013. Handwritten.

Cornelisse, Elizabeth. Unpublished essay. Montcalm CC., 21 Jan. 2013. Handwritten.

Dean, Pat. Telephone conversation. 14 Mar. 2013.

De La Fuente, Michael. Unpublished essay. Montcalm CC., 21 Jan. 2013. Handwritten.

Dept. of Veterans Affairs Medical Center of Battle Creek, MI. Letter to Ed Pusick. 16 Jun. 2000. Typewritten.

"Ed Pusick is Master of Disaster." *Shipwreck Journal* Spring/Summer 1992: 4, 7. Print.

Feltner, Charles E. and Jeri Baron Feltner. Shipwrecks of the Straits of Mackinac. Dearborn, MI: Seajay Publications, 1980. Print.

Feltner, Jeri Baron and Charles E. Message to the authors. 14 Mar. 2013. Email.

Flowers, Ryan. Unpublished essay. Montcalm CC., 21 Jan. 2013. Handwritten.

Garvon, Barbara. Unpublished essay. Montcalm CC., 21 Jan. 2013. Handwritten.

Grand Haven Coast Guard Station. Letter to Ed Pusick. 2 Aug. 1978. Typewritten.

Grand Rapids Lawyer. Letter to Ed Pusick. 5 May. 1987. Typewritten.

Hamilton, Stephanie. Unpublished essay. Montcalm CC., 21 Jan. 2013. Handwritten.

Harris, Chaley. Unpublished essay. Montcalm CC., 21 Jan. 2013. Handwritten.

Heden, Karl. *The Great Lakes Guide to Sunken Ships.* Boston: Brandon Books, 1993. Print.

Hill, Jeremy. Unpublished essay. Montcalm CC., 21 Jan. 2013. Handwritten.

Hill, Robert. Unpublished essay. Montcalm CC., 21 Jan. 2013. Handwritten.

Hedrick, Sydney. Unpublished essay. Montcalm CC., 21 Jan. 2013. Handwritten.

Hoogeveen, Sarin. Unpublished essay. Montcalm CC., 21 Jan. 2013. Handwritten.

Hopkins, Katlin. Unpublished essay. Montcalm CC., 21 Jan. 2013. Handwritten.

"James Davidson." Wrecks. Online. Internet. Retrieved 2012. http://www.wrecksite.eu.

Jensen, Ryan. Unpublished essay. Montcalm CC., 21 Jan. 2013. Handwritten.

"John M. Osborn." Great Lakes Shipwrecks. Online. Internet. Retrieved 2012. http://www.shipwreckmuseum.com.

Johnson, Carolyn. "Ed Pusick – Master of Disaster." Unpublished reflections. Montcalm CC Art Department, 4 Feb. 2013. Handwritten.

Kaat, Carrie. Unpublished essay. Montcalm CC., 21 Jan. 2013. Handwritten.

Iowa Author. Letter to Ed Pusick. 13 Oct. 1989. Typewritten.

Leete, Captain Frederick III. Letter to Ed Pusick. 21 June 2004. Typewritten.

Ley, Sean. Letter to Ed Pusick. 5 May. 1987. Typewritten.

Ley, Sean. Message to the authors. 20 Feb. 2013. Email.

Liebrock, Logann. Unpublished essay. Montcalm CC., 21 Jan. 2013. Handwritten.

Mangus, Kristine. Unpublished essay. Montcalm CC., 21 Jan. 2013. Handwritten.

McPharlin, Mike. Personal interview. 17 Dec. 2012.

Michigan Bureau of History. Letter to Ed Pusick. 26 July. 1988. Typewritten.

Michigan State University. Letter to Ed Pusick. 27 Feb. 1979. Typewritten.

Michigan State University. Letter to Ed Pusick. 22 Mar. 1979. Typewritten.

Mogg, Amber. Unpublished essay. Montcalm CC., 21 Jan. 2013. Handwritten.

Nelson, Katrina. Unpublished essay. Montcalm CC., 21 Jan. 2013. Handwritten.

Netzley, Marissa. Unpublished essay. Montcalm CC., 21 Jan. 2013. Handwritten.

Ogle, Travis. Unpublished essay. Montcalm CC., 21 Jan. 2013. Handwritten.

Paulen, Mackenzie. Unpublished essay. Montcalm CC., 21 Jan. 2013. Handwritten.

Pusick, Ed. "A Fond Remembrance." Unpublished essay. 10 Nov. 2004. Handwritten.

Pusick, Ed. "A Link to the Past." Unpublished essay. 28 Jun. 1998. Handwritten.

Pusick, Ed. "Devotion Versus Combat – A Sad Story." Unpublished narrative. N.d. Handwritten.

Pusick, Ed. "Expedition to the North Country." Unpublished essay. 10 Nov. 2004. Handwritten.

Pusick, Ed. Letter. N.d. Handwritten.

Pusick, Ed. Letter to George. N.d. Typewritten.

Pusick, Ed. Letter to Lois Hauck. N.d. Handwritten.

Pusick, Ed. Letter to Wyoming Library Board. 20 Oct. 1978. Handwritten.

Pusick, Ed. Letter to Michigan Dept. of Education. 15. Aug. 1982. Typewritten.

Pusick, Ed. Letter to WUOM Station Manager. 30 Jan. 1984. Typewritten.

Pusick, Ed. Letter to Fred Stonehouse. 21 Dec. 1987. Handwritten.

Pusick, Ed. Letter to Assistant Director, ---- Press. 12 Nov. 1990. Typewritten.

Pusick, Ed. Letter to Tom Farnquist. 5 Aug. 1992. Typewritten.

Pusick, Ed. Letter to Fred Stonehouse. 1 Sep. 1992. Typewritten.

Pusick, Ed. Letter to Vice Admiral, USBS. 7 Sep. 1992. Typewritten.

Pusick, Ed. Letter to Fred Stonehouse. 1 Oct. 1994. Typewritten.

Pusick, Ed. Letter to WNEM TV-5. 10 Jul. 1995. Typewritten.

Pusick, Ed. Letter to Lois Hauck. 18 Jun. 2003. Handwritten.

Pusick, Ed. Letter to Lois Hauck. 25 Aug. 2003. Handwritten.

Pusick, Ed. Letter to Lois Hauck. 8 Oct. 2003. Handwritten.

Pusick, Ed. Letter to Lois Hauck. 18 Oct. 2003. Handwritten.

Pusick, Ed. Letter. 9 Nov. 2003. Typewritten.

Pusick, Ed. Letter to "Lord of the Manor." 10 Nov. 2003. Typewritten.

Pusick, Ed. Letter to Lois Hauck. 28 Nov. 2003. Handwritten.

Pusick, Ed. Letter to Lois Hauck. 12 Dec. 2003. Handwritten.

Pusick, Ed. Letter to Lois Hauck. 18 Dec. 2003. Handwritten.

Pusick, Ed. Letter to Lois Hauck. 12 Jan. 2004. Handwritten.

Pusick, Ed. Letter to Lois Hauck. 21 Dec. 2004. Handwritten.

Pusick, Ed. Letter to Lois Hauck. 16 Oct. 2004. Handwritten.

Pusick, Ed. Letter to Lois Hauck. 5 Nov. 2004. Handwritten.

Pusick, Ed. Letter to a friend. 5 Dec. 2005. Typewritten.

Pusick, Ed. Letter to Lois Hauck. 9 Jan. 2005. Handwritten.

Pusick, Ed. Letter to Lois Hauck. 4 Feb. 2005. Handwritten.

Pusick, Ed. Letter to Lois Hauck. 11 Feb. 2005. Handwritten.

Pusick, Ed. "First Designs." Unpublished essay. N.d. Typewritten.

Pusick, Ed. "Rouse Simmons – A Yuletide Legacy." Unpublished essay. N.d. Handwritten.

Pusick, Ed. "Ships and Sailors." Unpublished essay. 12 Dec. 1981. Handwritten.

Pusick, Ed. "Some Things Tend to Resurface." Unpublished essay. 14 May 2004. Handwritten.

Pusick, Ed. "The Glorious Dream." Unpublished poem. N.d. Typewritten.

Rademacker, Tom. "Great Ones Not Always Appreciated Until They're Gone." The Grand Rapids Press [MI] 30 Apr. 2006, B1-B2. Print.

Rish, Taylor. Unpublished essay. Montcalm CC., 21 Jan. 2013. Handwritten.

Shipwreck Journal (cover) Summer 1992: 1. Print.

"Society Notes Passing of Artist Edward Pusick." Shipwreck Journal Spring/Summer 2006: 7. Print.

State of Michigan Dept. of Natural Resources. Letter to Ed Pusick. 7 Sep. 1978. Typewritten.

"Steamer Superior." Maritime History of the Great Lakes. Online. Internet. Retrieved 2012. http://images.maritimehistoryofthegreatlakes.ca.

Stone, Barb. Letter to Ed Pusick. 26 Oct. 2004. Typewritten.

Stonehouse, Frederick. Haunted Lakes: Great Lakes Ghost Stories, Superstitions and Sea Serpents. Duluth, MN: Lake Superior Port Cities, Inc., 1997. Print.

Stonehouse, Frederick. Message to authors. 27 Jan. 2013. Email.

Stonehouse, Frederick. *Munising Shipwrecks.* Marquette: Shipwrecks
    Unlimited, 1980. Print.

Stonehouse, Frederick. *The Maritime Prints of Edward Pusick.*
    [promotional brochure] Marquette: Shipwrecks Unlimited,
    n.d. Print.

Sweet, Jace. Unpublished essay. Montcalm CC., 21 Jan. 2013.
    Handwritten.

"The Edmund Fitzgerald." *Great Lakes Shipwrecks.* Online. Internet.
    Retrieved 2012. http://www.shipwreckmuseum.com.

"The Herman H. Hettler" *Munising Bay Shipwreck Tours.* Online.
    Internet. Retrieved 2012.
    http://shipwrecktours.com/shipwrecks/the-herman-hettler.

Tower Productions of Chicago. Letter to Ed Pusick. 25 May. 1999.
    Typewritten.

Trystad, Danielle. Unpublished essay. Montcalm CC., 21 Jan. 2013.
    Handwritten.

VanPatten, Shane. Unpublished essay. Montcalm CC., 21 Jan. 2013.
    Handwritten.

Veltkamp, Randi. Unpublished essay. Montcalm CC., 21 Jan. 2013.
    Handwritten.

Walsh, Emily. Unpublished essay. Montcalm CC., 21 Jan. 2013.
    Handwritten.

Wierde, Jared. Unpublished essay. Montcalm CC., 21 Jan. 2013.
    Handwritten.

Wucher, Andrew. Unpublished essay. Montcalm CC., 21 Jan. 2013.
    Handwritten.

Wyoming MI Library Board. Letter to Ed Pusick. 27 Sep. 1978.
    Typewritten.

About the Authors

Lois T. Hauck holds a Bachelor of Science degree from Baptist Bible College of PA, is a home-health caregiver for Comfort Keepers in Grand Rapids, MI, and serves as a volunteer for the Ronald McDonald House. Also an artist, she served as Ed Pusick's caregiver for five years with an appreciation for his shipwreck drawings and other illustrations as well as the stories behind them. She was the one who discovered his lifeless body, and endeavors to keep his memory and works in the public arena. Lois is also the author of *The Caregiver,* and is a co-author with her husband, Gary, of *Spiritual Formation.*

Gary L. Hauck has a Doctor of Philosophy degree from Michigan State University, and serves as the Dean of Instruction and Student Development at Montcalm Community College in Sidney, MI, where he also teaches Humanities. He is a member of the Montcalm Area Art Association and the Mid-Michigan Arts Council, and serves as President of the Montcalm Area Humanities Council. Gary also serves on the boards of the Flat River Historical Museum in Greenville, MI, and the Heritage Village Association in Sidney. He is the author of *Exploring Humanities around the World,* and *The Story of Heritage Village.*

The Haucks have been married for over 40 years and have four children: Heidi, Greg (and Rachel), Andrew (and Becky), and Jared. They also have two grandchildren: Jacob and Liliana, born to Greg and Rachel. Lois and Gary reside in Grand Rapids, MI.

You may contact the authors at:

Lois Hauck (loisth17@gmail.com)

and/or

Gary Hauck (gary49525@hotmail.com)